HOME DISTILLING HANDBOOK

**Christopher G. Yorke, M. Ed
Mason Creek Publishing**

Home Distilling Handbook
By Christopher G. Yorke, M. Ed

Published by:
Mason Creek Publishing
35111 NE 94th Ave.
La Center, WA 98629
(360)263-5780
cyorke57@gmail.com

All rights reserved. No part of this book may be reproduced or transmitted in any form or by any means, electronic or mechanical, including photocopying, recording, or by any information storage and retrieval system, without written permission from the publisher.

Copyright 2017 by Mason Creek Publishing

ISBN 978-1978458109
Printed in the United States of America
Library of Congress CIP Data Pending

Money Back Guarantee
If the Home Distilling Handbook does not meet your expectations for any reason, return it to Mason Creek Publishing for a 100% refund. Book must be returned in good condition within 30 days of purchase date. Be sure to include your return address.

TESTIMONIALS

Comments made by people who have consumed spirits made using the procedures in the Home Distilling Handbook.

"This stuff is as good as you said it was."
  - Dave Carlile, Yacolt, WA

"The single malt is beautiful whiskey."
  - Fred Chappelle, The Philippines

"We love it."
  - Alex Collins, Portland, OR

"A very unique flavor with exceptional quality."
  - Tod Garred, Battle Ground, WA

"It's an olfactory sensation."
  - Tim Hicks, Brush Prairie, WA

"The single malt whiskey is like drinking silk."
  - Kevin Kernen, Vancouver, WA

"The bourbon has a very rich flavor."
  - Jerry Klug, Brush Prairie, WA

"The smokey bourbon has an especially good smooth taste."
  - Steve McNeal, Battle Ground, WA

"It's amazing."
  - Josh Simpson, Vancouver, WA

"The single malt was surprisingly smooth."
  - Jason Susee, Vancouver, WA

"I took a bottle of bourbon to a party and I only got one shot out of it!"
  - Jason Susee, Vancouver, WA

Home Distilling Handbook Contents

INTRODUCTION x

CHAPTER 1 - WHISKEY BASICS 1

TYPES OF SPIRITS 1
Bourbon 2
Corn Whiskey 2
Moonshine 2
Rum 3
Rye Whiskey 3
Single Malt Whiskey (Scotch style) 3
Tennessee Whiskey 4
Vodka 4

GRAIN 4
Grain Anatomy 5
Glucose, Maltose, Maltotriose 5
Barley 6
Barley Malt 6
Peat and Peated Barley 7
Corn 7
Oats 7
Rye 7
Wheat 8
Grain Bill 8

CHAPTER 2 - EQUIPMENT, SUPPLIES, SETUP, AND USE 9

Alembic Pot Still and Parts 10
Condenser Parts and Setup 11
Condenser Coiled Copper Tubing 12
Alcohol Parrot 12
Alcohol Parrot and Distillate Collection Jar Setup 13
Alcoholometer (Alcohol Hydrometer) 13

How to use an Alcoholometer (Alcohol Hydrometer) 14
Adjusting ABV for temperatures above or below 60°F 14
Saccharometer (Sugar Hydrometer) 18
Reading Specific Gravity and Potential Alcohol 18
Specific Gravity and Potential Alcohol Chart 20
Graduated Cylinder 21
15 Gallon Cooking Pot with Lid 22
Food Grade Long Stem Thermometer 22
Large Wooden Stirring Paddle 23
Propane Burner - for cooking mash 23
5 Gallon Propane Tank 23
Electric Hot Plate Burner - for distilling 24
8 Ounce Canning Jars 24
1 Gallon Aging Jars 25
Aging Jar Labels 25
Distiller's Active Dry Yeast (DADY) 27
Yeast Nutrients 28
Amylase Enzyme 28
American White Oak Cubes - Toasted or Charred 28
Home Made American White Oak Aging Cubes 29
Propane Torch Charring 30
Propane Camp Stove Charring 31
Charring Times 32
12 Gallon Fermenting Bucket with Lid 33
Mash Bag 34
Food Scale 35
Large Plastic Bowl 35
Kitchen Strainer 35
Flour for Sealing the Still Head 36
Turkey Baster 37
Fermentation Chamber (Optional) 38
Homemade Mash Press 39
Wort Chiller 40
pH Meter 40
Duct Tape 41
Product Record 42
Miscellaneous Supplies 45

CHAPTER 3 - MAKING WHISKEY............47

The Grain Bill..47
Example Bourbon Grain Bill..48
How to Calculate Total Mash Volume Needed.................48
Basic Structure of the Whiskey Recipes 49
How to Calculate Required Grain Quantities...................50

THE MASH...51
Steps for Cooking the Mash 52
Place Water into your Cooking Pot 52
Heat the Water...52
Add Corn and Gelatinize 52
Add Remaining Grains 53
Add Amylase Enzyme 53
Check the pH of the Mash 53
Rest the Mash 54
Cool the Mash..54
Check the Specific Gravity of the Wort 55

FERMENTATION 56
FERMENTING ON THE GRAIN 56
Check the pH of the Mash 56
Sanitize Fermentation Equipment 57
Place the Mash Bag into the Fermentation Bucket 57
Add Yeast Nutrients 57
Pitch the Yeast..58
Aerate the Mash...59
Pour Mash into the Fermentation Bucket 60
Put the Lid on the Fermentation Bucket and Label it.........60
Put Fermentation Bucket into Fermentation Chamber......61
Procedures During Fermentation.......................................62
Check for Grain Cap and Crackling Sound 62
Check the Temperature if the Fermentation Chamber 62
Check the Specific Gravity of the Wash 63

RECOVERING THE WASH 65
Open the Fermentation Bucket and Tie a Rope
Around the Top Part of the Mash Bag..............................65

Pull the Fermentation Bucket Underneath 4X4 Beam 66
Pull Mash Bag Up and Tie to 4X4 66
Press Out Wash 68

FERMENTING OFF THE GRAIN 69
Cool the Mash 69
Sanitize Fermentation Equipment 69
Separate the Wort from the Mash 69
Tie the Mash Bag Up to the 4X4 Beam 70
Press Out Remaining Wort 70
Sparge the Mash (optional) 70
Pour All of the Wort into the Fermentation Bucket 71
Check Specific Gravity of the Wort 71
Check pH of the Wort 72
Add Yeast Nutrients 72
Pitch the Yeast 72
Aerate the Wort 73
Place Fermentation Bucket into Fermentation Chamber ... 73
Procedures During Fermentation 73

STRIPPING RUN - FIRST DISTILLATION 74
Remove the Wash from the Fermentation Bucket 74
Pour the Wash into the Still 75
Attach Head to the Still and Lyne Arm to Condenser 75
Seal the Still Head with Flour Paste 76
Set Up 1 Gallon Collection Jar and Alcohol Parrot 76
Turn on Burner 78
Turn on Condenser Water Line 78
Collect Distillate 79
Example Stripping Run Data Table 80-81

SPIRIT RUN - SECOND DISTILLATION 83
Clean the Still 85
Put Line of Duct Tape on Table 86
Get 8 oz. Mason Jars Ready 86
Pour Low Wines into Still 87
Put Still Back Together 87
Turn on Condenser Water Line 87
Set Up Foreshots Collection Jar 88

Turn on Burner 88
Collect Foreshots 89
Put Alcohol Parrot and First Jar in Place 89
Collect Distillate in 4 oz. Quantities and Record Date 90
Stopping the Spirit Run 91
Making the Cuts 92
Separate Out the Hearts 94
Example Spirit Run Data Table 96-97

AGING YOUR WHISKEY 99
Proof Down Your Whiskey 99
Pour Whiskey into Aging Jar 100
Add Toasted or Charred White Oaks Cubes to Jar 100
Label the Jar 101

BOTTLING YOUR WHISKEY 102
Proof Whiskey Down to your Desired Drinking Proof ... 102
Rinse Out your Bottles 102
Filter your Whiskey into Bottles 102
Put Cork in Bottles 102
Attach Label to Bottles 102

CHAPTER 4 - RECIPES 105

Straight Bourbon 105
Smokey Bourbon 105
Wheated Bourbon 106
Single Malt Whiskey (Scotch style) 106
Irish Whisky 106
Oat Whiskey 107
Rye Whiskey 107
Corn Whiskey 107
Chocolate Malt Whiskey 107
Basic Corn Moonshine 108
Corn and Sugar Moonshine 108
Malted Barley Moonshine 108
Sweet Feed Moonshine 109
Oat Moonshine 109

Instructions for Making Moonshine 109
Winter Wheat Vodka 109
Instructions for Making Vodka..110
Rum..110
Instructions for Making Rum..111
Sour Mash Whiskey...111

CHAPTER 5 - CLEANING AND SANITIZING YOUR EQUIPMENT...............112

CHAPTER 6 - SAFETY GUIDELINES 114

EXPANDED GLOSSARY 115-127
The expanded glossary includes alphabetized terms and concepts that are explained in much greater detail than a standard glossary.

APPENDIX 128
Appendix A - Spirit Run Graphic 129
Appendix B - Summarized Whiskey
             Making Instructions 130
Appendix C - Equipment and Supply List Summary 134
Appendix D - Home Distillery Setup Picture 136

INDEX 137-40

ABOUT THE AUTHOR..141

INTRODUCTION

The purpose of the Home Distilling Handbook is to get you up and running now. Everything you need to know is in the book. You won't need to read four different books or spend countless hours searching the internet for the information you need - it is ALL here. There are many different approaches to distilling alcohol and making whiskey. This manual contains the basic concepts and the proven procedures you need in order to successfully make your own spirits, including clear pictures of every step. After you master the basic processes outlined in the book you can begin to venture out and try new methods and create your own unique whiskey. I recommend that you read through chapters 1 and 2 first in order to get a good general overview of the whiskey making process and all of the supplies and equipment you will be using. I also think it would be a good idea to read through the expanded glossary. Then, in chapter 3 we will get into the detailed steps and procedures of cooking mash, fermentation, distilling, aging, and bottling. The first 2 chapters may seem a little overwhelming at first. Just push through them and when you get into the later chapters things will start to gel and you will be prepared to make top shelf spirits. Although the concepts covered in the book can be applied to the use of any kind of still, we will be illustrating the use of a copper alembic pot still. It is the oldest type of still, but still considered by many to produce the best, most flavorful whiskey. It is also a good type of still to use when learning the whiskey making process.

Please remember that in order to distill spirits legally you need a license. For a small distiller you can apply for a craft distiller's license. You will need to apply for a Federal license and check with the requirements of your particular State.

CHAPTER 1

Whiskey Basics

The information presented in this chapter is designed to give you an overview of the whiskey making process. Read it over and don't worry about trying to memorize the information. In later chapters we will go through an example batch of bourbon and learn every part of the process in a step-by-step fashion.

WHISKEY

The word whiskey comes from the Latin word "aqua vitae," meaning the water of life. Whiskey is a distilled spirit made from fermented grain or any other organic matter containing carbohydrates. The distillate is aged in charred white oak barrels to produce whiskey. Remember that whiskey is a general term for various types of distilled spirits including bourbon, Scotch Whisky, Tennessee whiskey, Canadian whiskey and Irish whiskey.

    Let us start with a short description of how whiskey is made. First, a mixture of grains, or other organic biomass, is mixed with water and cooked to form a mash. The mash is cooled and yeast is added so that sugars in the mash can be converted into alcohol (fermentation). The resulting fermented liquid (wash), which now contains alcohol, is heated in order to separate the various kinds of alcohol out of the wash (distillation). The distillate is aged with charred or toasted oak to produce whiskey. Again, this is a very short description. We will get deeper into the process as we proceed. Also note that this process is basically the same, with some variations, for Tennessee whiskey, bourbon, rum, vodka and single malt whiskey, (Scotch Whisky style) and moonshine.

TYPES OF SPIRITS

There are obviously many more kinds of spirits than the ones included in this book. The spirits I have described are those that I have experience with and work very well for home distilling.

Bourbon

The grain bill for bourbon is corn, barley and rye. It must be at least 51% corn. Most commercial bourbons are made from 70-80% corn, 15-20% barley malt and 5-10% rye. Bourbon must be aged a minimum of 2 years in new charred American White Oak barrels.

Corn Whiskey

The grain bill for corn whiskey must contain at least 80% corn. The remaining 20% is usually malted barley. Corn whiskey must be aged for a minimum of two years in new or used white oak barrels. The barrels don't have to be charred. Corn whiskey is often marketed as "White Lightening."

Irish Whiskey

Irish whiskey is obviously made in Ireland. The grain bill is 50% barley and 50% barley malt. Irish whiskey is normally **fermented off the grain**. The big difference is that Irish whiskey is triple distilled. Three distillations give the final product a very clean taste. It is aged in charred white oak barrels.

Moonshine

Moonshine is illegal whiskey made at home. Moonshine can be made of just about any organic material that can be fermented and distilled, but the most common type of moonshine is made of corn mash. To make a long story short, moonshine is simply ethanol that has been illegally distilled, has a high proof, and is not aged. In order to achieve the high proof that moonshine is famous for, usually 150 to 180 proof, moonshiners would distill a batch three times. After each distillation they would mark an "X" on the jug to keep track. Back during the days of prohibition, between 1920 and 1933, the production and sale of liquor (spirits) was illegal in the United States. People would illegally distill spirits at night, in the "shine of the moon," to avoid being caught by the law. The term is thought to have originated in England. Early English whiskey smugglers were called "Moonrakers" because they worked by the light of the moon. You can find whiskey called Moonshine in liquor stores, but it is not actually moonshine. It is simply white dog (white whiskey) that has not been aged in an oak barrel and it (is) made legally. All distilled spirits start off as plain old ethanol, including moonshine. The various kinds of alcohol, including ethanol, come out of the still as clear as water.

Rum

Rum is made from sugar and/or molasses. There are three main types of rum: white, gold and dark. White rum is not aged and it is filtered which removes much of the color and flavor. Gold rum is also known as amber rum. It is aged in charred white oak barrels. Dark rum is aged in charred white oak barrels for a longer period of time. Caramelized sugar is often added to add color and flavor.

Rye Whiskey

American rye whiskey must be made with at least 51% rye in the mash. Other grains usually include barley malt as a source of enzymes needed for saccharification. American rye whiskey is very different than Canadian rye which is made with a high percentage of corn in the mash. Straight rye whiskey must be aged for at least two years in charred new Amercian white oak barrels and cannot be blended with other batches. Rye whiskey has a spicier and fruitier taste than bourbon.

Single Malt Whiskey (Scotch Whisky in Scotland)

To be called Scotch, whisky needs to be made in Scotland. Scotch is made from 100% malted barley. Some Scotches also have some peated barley in the mash. This gives the Scotch whisky the smoky or peaty flavor. Single malt whiskey's are normally fermented off the grain. Scotch is aged a minimum of three years in charred white oak barrels. The best Scotch is made from a single batch of malted barley and not blended with any other batch. This is called single malt whisky. In America whiskey made from 100% malted barley is called Single Malt Whiskey since it can't be called Scotch.

Tennessee Whiskey

Tennessee whiskey is basically bourbon, but it has been charcoal mellowed. That means it has been slowly seeped through a vat of sugar maple charcoal before going into an aging barrel. The addition of this step in the process makes it illegal to call the whiskey "bourbon." An example is Jack Daniel's Tennessee Whiskey.

Vodka

The name vodka comes from the Russian word "voda" which means water. The official definition for vodka is that it is a neutral spirit without distinctive character, aroma, taste or color. Although different vodkas do have subtle differences in aroma and taste. This is due to the variety of items that can be used to make it and differences in the actual distillation process. It is usually distilled using a continuous column still which produces a more refined pure ethanol. Vodka is usually distilled at least three times, especially if using a pot still. It is also filtered using activated carbon to further purify the distillate. Vodka can be made from anything that can be fermented as opposed to whiskey which must be made from grain. Most vodkas are made from grains or potatoes. Most commercial vodka distilleries make their finest vodkas from winter wheat. Vodka is not aged in barrels like whiskey, although it will mellow with time. It is distilled, filtered and bottled.

GRAIN

Grain refers to the seed produced by plants in the grass family (gramineae). Most distilled spirits are made from grains including corn, barley, rye, wheat, oats and triticale. Although spirits can be made from pretty much any kind of organic matter containing carbohydrates, the grains are the most popular.

Grain Anatomy

It is important to have a basic knowledge of grain anatomy in order to understand how alcohol is produced from fermented grains. Refer to the picture below as we discuss grain anatomy. This diagram shows a generic example of a grain (seed). It could be barley, rye, oats, or wheat. Although corn is also in the gramineae family, its structure is a little different than the other grains. The endosperm contains starch (carbohydrates). It is the white material that makes up the largest part of popcorn. When water enters the seed, enzymes are activated that convert the starch to glucose (simple sugar). The embryo (germ), which is an immature plant, feeds on the glucose and water, and begins to grow (germination). When we cook our mash we are allowing the natural enzymes in the grain, plus additional enzymes we add, to convert the starch into glucose. This is the process of saccharification. After the mash cools we add yeast which consumes the glucose (fermentation). As the yeast ferments the glucose it produces alcohol and carbon dioxide.

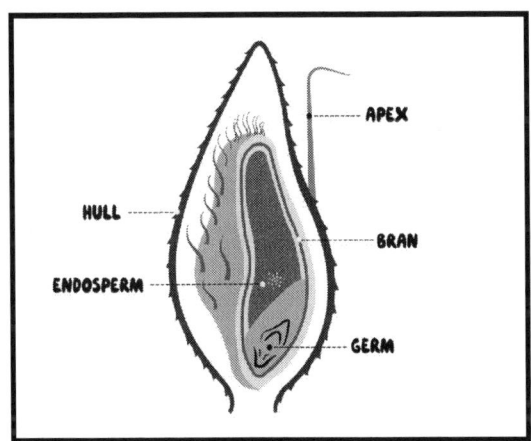

Glucose, Maltose, Maltotriose

Glucose, maltose and maltotriose are the main components of the starches found in the endosperm of cereal grains. Glucose ($C_6H_{12}O_6$) is the simplest sugar and is known as a monosaccharide meaning one glucose molecule. Maltose ($C_{12}H_{22}O_{11}$) is a disaccharide with two glucose molecules. Maltotriose ($C_{18}H_{32}O_{16}$) is a trisaccharide consisting of three glucose molecules. These sugars are present in the wort and are used by the yeasts during the process of fermentation.

Barley

The scientific name for barley is Hordeum vulgare. There are two main varieties, 2 row and 6 row. Two row barley has 2 rows of grain kernels on each head. It has a lower protein content, but higher carbohydrate (starch) content. This is the primary kind used to make barley malt. Six row barley has 6 rows of grain kernels per head. It has more protein and a lower carbohydrate content. It is primarily used as livestock feed.

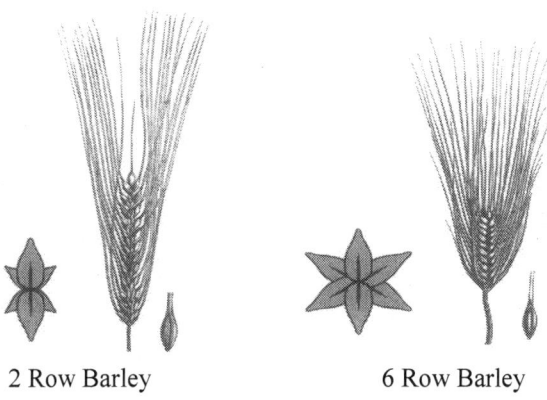

2 Row Barley   6 Row Barley

The difference between a head of 2-row barley and a head of 6-row barley is the arrangement of the kernels when you look at the head of barley down its axis.

Barley Malt

Barley malt or malted barley, is made by soaking barley in water and initiating the germination (sprouting) process. The grain is then heated with hot air in order to stop germination. During this partial germination beta-amylase enzyme is produced inside the grain that helps convert starches in the grain into simple sugars like maltose and glucose. When malted barley is mixed with other grains in the mash the beta-amylase enzyme, plus alpha-amylase enzyme added by the distiller, converts all of the starches from all of the different grains in the mash into glucose. Malted grains, like malted barley, are often referred to as malt, referring to the maltose in the grain.

Peat and Peated Barley

Peat consists of dead plant material including moss, grasses and tree roots that have been compacted under a layer of soil and decomposed slowly over many years, sometimes thousands of years. The peat is dug up, dried and can be burned for fuel or other uses. In whiskey making, especially Scotch, peat is burned underneath a layer of malted barley. The heat from the burning peat stops the germination of the malted barley and dries it out. The peat smoke produces chemicals called phenols that are absorbed by the malted barley and give it a smoky flavor. Peated barley is often used in making Scotch or other malt whiskeys. Regular malted barley is dried without using peat and does not have the smoky smell or flavor.

Corn

The scientific name for corn is Zea mays. There are 6 different types of corn in the Zea mays genus that are produced and used by humans, dent corn, flint corn, pod corn, popcorn, flour corn and sweet corn. Yellow dent corn (Zea mays var. indentata) is the primary corn used for ethanol and therefore whiskey production. Yellow dent corn has a high starch content compared to other varieties and that characteristic makes it good for making spirits.

Oats

Oats, Avena sativa, are used to make bread, oatmeal, other baked goods and as livestock feed. There are a few distillers who make oat whiskey. The grain bill is usually 85% oats and 15% barley malt. Oats create a very smooth whiskey with a mellow, sweet, toasted grain flavor.

Rye

Rye is another cereal grain in the gramineae family. It's scientific name is Secale cereale. Rye is used to make flour, rye bread, rye beer, whiskey, vodka and is also used as livestock feed. Rye can be used to make rye whiskey, is part of the grain bill in bourbon, and is often used in making Canadian whiskey. It provides a spicy flavor to the whiskey. Early whiskey's in the United States were primarily made of rye since it was grown extensively at the time and was cheap. As the production of other grains like corn increased, other types of whiskey became more popular.

Wheat

Wheat, Triticum aestivum, is the second most produced grain in the world, topped only by corn. There are only a few straight wheat whiskeys produced in the world. However, there are many whiskeys which are "wheated," meaning that a small percentage of the grain bill includes wheat. Wheat tends to make whiskey smoother and sweeter tasting. The flavor profile of wheat whiskey is much milder than whiskey without wheat.

Grain Bill

In the distilling industry the grain bill is simply a list of which grains are used to make the mash and the percentage of each. For example, the grain bill for Jack Daniels Tennessee Whiskey is 80% corn, 12% rye and 8% malted barley. Of course, trying to make Jack Daniels whiskey isn't just a matter of using their grain bill. They use various techniques in their production process that produces the unique flavors of Jack Daniels, techniques that are closely guarded secrets.

CHAPTER 2

**Equipment
Supplies
Setup
Use
Cost
Where to Purchase**

ALEMBIC POT STILL, PARTS AND SETUP

The copper alembic pot still is the oldest type of still used. Many people, including some commercial distilleries, believe the Alembic Copper Still produces the best tasting whiskey. It consists of the still, still head, lyne arm, vapor thermometer, condenser, and coiled condenser tubing, (goes down into the condenser). The wash is placed into the still and heated by the burner for distillation. Alcohol vapors accumulate in the still head, travel past the vapor thermometer and into the condenser tubing. As the vapor travels down the condenser tubing into the condenser, the cool water in the condenser converts the vapor back into liquid. The liquefied alcohol exits the condenser through the food-grade condenser discharge tube and goes into a distillate collection jar. I recommend buying a 35 liter (9 Gal.) still. All of my examples in this book will relate to using a 35 liter still. You can purchase one from Iberian Copper's (copper-alembic.com) for about $300 plus shipping.

A - 35 liter still
B - Still head
C - Vapor thermometer
D - Lyne Arm
E - Condenser
F - Food grade discharge tube
G - Burner
H - Alcohol Parrot
I - Distillate collection jar

CONDENSER PARTS AND SETUP

The condenser consists of a copper bucket with a coiled copper tube that brings the vaporized distillate from the still down through a supply of cool water. As the vapor enters the coiled copper tubing, which is in the cool water, the vapor returns to a liquid and drains out through the food grade tubing into your distillate collection jar.

- A - Water line in, 1/2" black irrigation tubing, with 1/2" hose clamp. Brings water into condenser bucket.
- B - Water line out, 1/2" black irrigation tubing, with 1/2" hose clamp. A long enough pipe to go outside to drain.
- C - 1/2" food grade tubing connected with 1/2" hose clamp. For distillate outflow to collection jar.

CONDENSER COILED COPPER TUBING

Inside the condenser you find the coiled condenser tubing. During distillation the condenser is full of cool water that continuously flows into the condenser from an inflow line and leaves the condenser through an outflow line. This provides the cool water required to convert the alcohol vapors back into liquid form.

ALCOHOL PARROT

The alcohol parrot is used to monitor the alcohol by volume (ABV) coming out of the still during distillation. This is very useful because you can watch the ABV continuously as you distill. The setup for the parrot is shown on the next page. You can purchase a parrot for about $35.00 from ebay.

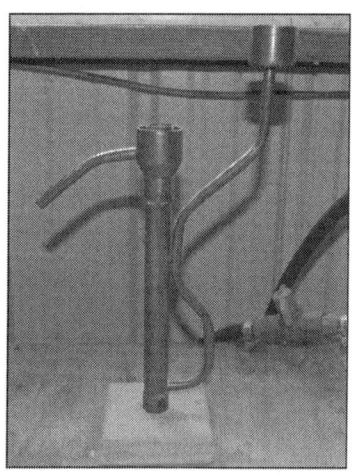

ALCOHOL PARROT AND DISTILLATE COLLECTION JAR SETUP

The alcohol parrot collects distillate from the food grade distillate tube (A) The alcohol hydrometer is placed into the parrot tube (B). Once the distillate has filled the parrot tube, ABV can be read off of the hydrometer. See "how to use an alcohol hydrometer" on page 14. Distillate flows out of the parrot and into the collection jar.

Alcoholometer (alcohol hydrometer)

The alcoholometer, measures the specific gravity of the distillate. Once you know the specific gravity you can determine the ABV. Specific gravity indicates how dense a liquid is. Alcohol is less dense than water so the hydrometer will float higher in it compared to water. The picture above shows you how the hydrometer is placed into the alcohol parrot. See page 14 for a complete explanation of how the hydrometer works and how to use it. You can purchase an alcohol hydrometer form brew stores or from Amazon.com for about $12.00.

HOW TO USE AN ALCOHOLOMETER (ALCOHOL HYDROMETER)

The alcohol hydrometer has two scales, one on each side. One side shows the abv percentage and the other shows the proof. Proof is simply twice the abv. For example, 40% abv is 80 proof.

When you place the hydrometer into a parrot, graduated cylinder, or any other receptacle it will float and you can read the abv or proof. If your reading was as shown with the arrow on the next page, you would have an abv of 45% and a proof of 90.

Each increment on the abv scale is 1.
Each increment on the proof scale is 2.

Reading at the meniscus. This is very important. The meniscus is the curved upper surface of a liquid in a tube. When you place the hydrometer into the distillate a meniscus will form around it. Make sure you read at the bottom of the meniscus, not at the part that rises up on the side of the hydrometer. The picture below shows how to read the proof on an alcohol hydrometer correctly. In this case the correct reading would be 164 proof.

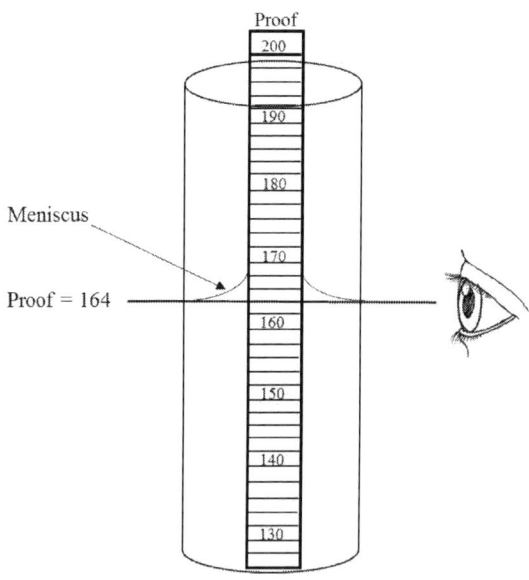

Reading the Alcoholometer

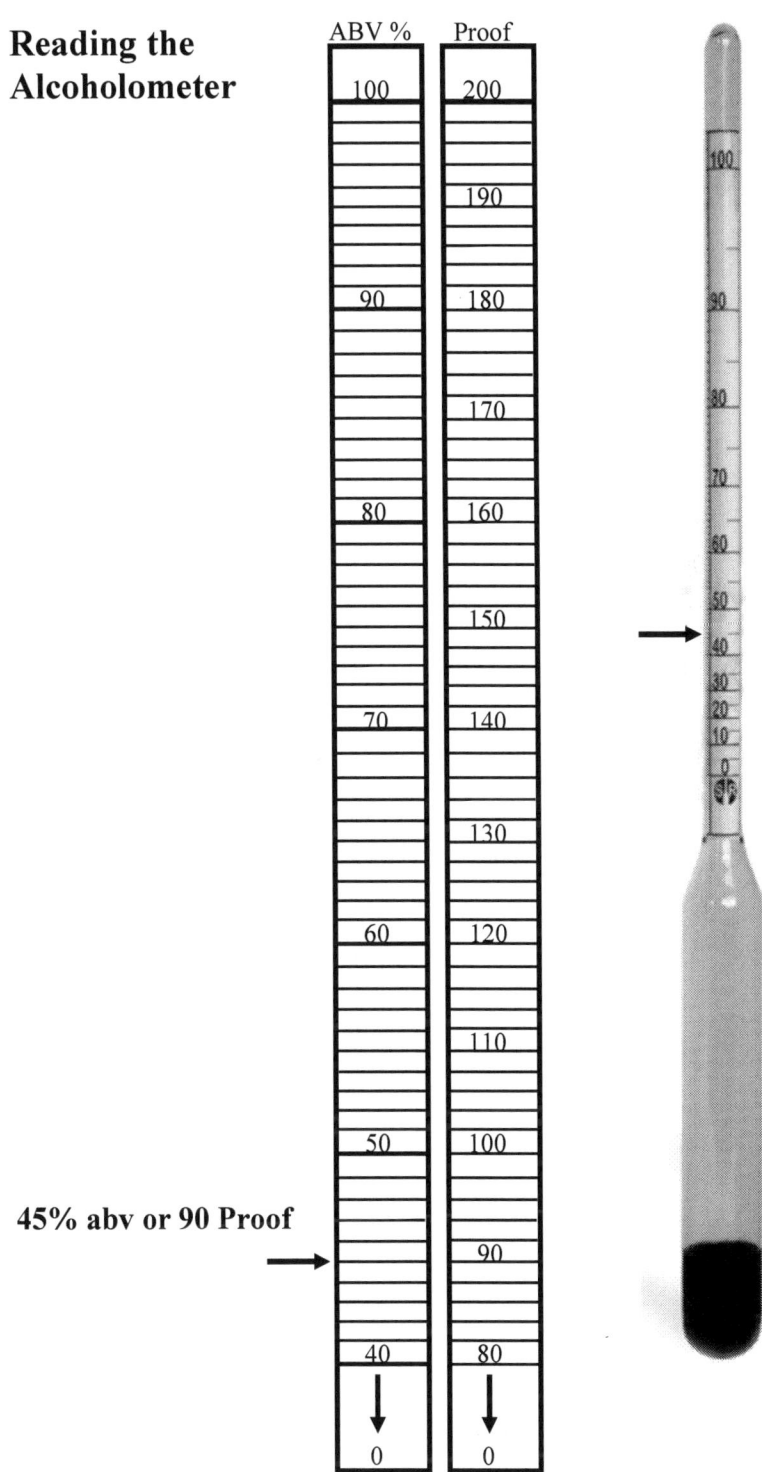

45% abv or 90 Proof

AJUSTING THE ABV FOR TEMPERATURES ABOVE OR BELOW 15.5°C (60°F).

The alcohol hydrometer is calibrated to work at 15.5°C (60°F). If the temperature of your distillate is above or below 15.5°C (60°F) you need to make an adjustment to your reading. As the distillate temperature increases the alcohol becomes less dense, the hydrometer sinks lower into the distillate and you get a false high reading. You need to subtract from the hydrometer reading in order to get the correct abv. As the distillate temperature decreases the alcohol becomes more dense, the hydrometer rises and you get a false low reading. You need to add to the hydrometer reading in order to get the correct abv. The chart on page 17 shows you the amounts to add or subtract at the various distillate temperatures. Make sure you check the <u>distillate temperature</u> and don't use the ambient air temperature when making these adjustments. Check the distillate temperature by inserting your long stem thermometer into your parrot tube.

Subtract from the abv reading when the distillate temperature is above 60°F.
Add to the abv reading when the distillate temperature is below 60°F.

(Photocopy the chart and post it on the wall next to your still.)

ABV TEMPERATURE CORRECTION

Temp °F	0-25 Proof	25-50 Proof	50-200 Proof
100	-14	-12	-16
95	-12	-10.5	-14
90	-10	-9	-12
85	-8.5	-7.5	-10
80	-7	-6	-8
75	-5	-4.5	-6
70	-3	-3	-4
65	-1.5	-1.5	-2
60	0	0	0
55	+1.5	+1.5	+2
50	+3.5	+3	+4
45	+5	+4.5	+6
40	+7	+6	+8
35	+9	+8	+10
30	+10.5	+9	+12
25	+12	+10.5	+14
20	+14	+12	+16
15	+16	+13.5	+18
10	+18	+15	+20
5	+19	+16.5	+22
0	+21	+18	+24

SUGAR HYDROMETER (SACCHAROMETER)

A saccharometer is a hydrometer used for determining the amount of sugar in a solution. In the case of making whiskey, the sugar hydrometer is used to measure the specific gravity (SG) in the mash, and the wash after fermentation is complete. Once we know the SG of the mash or the wash we can use the chart on page 20 to figure out the sugar content. We use this information to determine the potential alcohol in the mash and the wash. Potential alcohol (PA) is an estimate of the percentage of the mash or wash that will become alcohol from fermentation by the yeast. The sugar hydrometer has two scales, a specific gravity scale and a potential alcohol scale. The diagram on the right shows each scale. You can check the SG on the scale and also read the corresponding PA scale. It is more accurate however, to read the SG and use the chart on page 20 to identify the PA. When you purchase a sugar hydrometer a small version of the chart comes with it. A saccharometer can be purchased from a brew store or from Amazon.com for about $12.00.

READING THE SG AND PA

The more sugar that is in the mash or the wash the higher the SG will be. This means the density of the solution is higher. The higher the SG the higher the hydrometer will float in the solution. This will show a higher SG and PA reading on the hydrometer. As an example, look at the saccharometer on page 19. The correct reading would be 1.070 for SG and 9.20 percent for PA. Again, using the chart on page 20 will give you a more accurate reading.

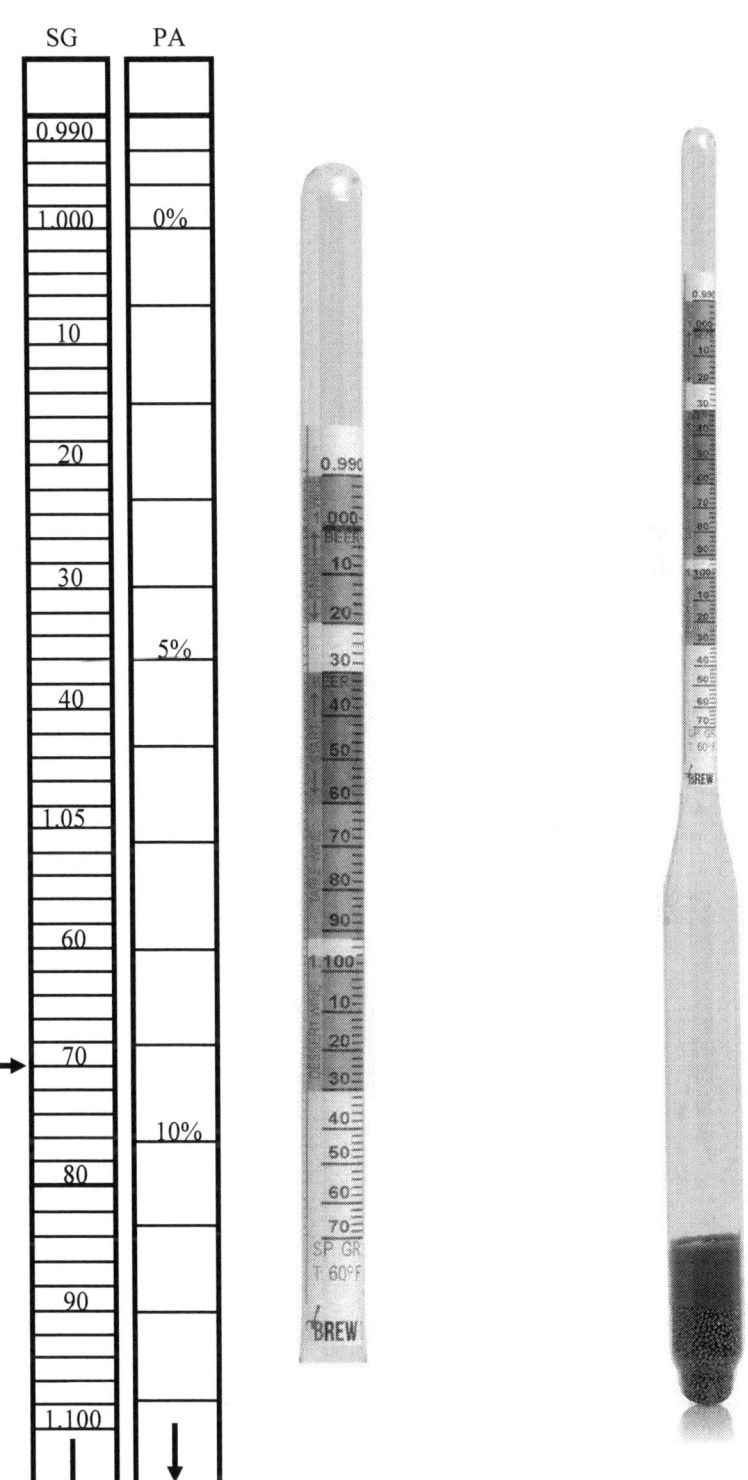

Specific Gravity and Potential Alcohol Chart

Specific Gravity (20°C/68°F)	Potential Alcohol (%/Volume)
1.000	0.0
1.005	0.7
1.010	1.3
1.015	2.0
1.020	2.6
1.025	3.3
1.030	4.0
1.035	4.6
1.040	5.3
1.045	5.9
1.050	6.6
1.055	7.2
1.060	7.9
1.065	8.6
1.070	9.2
1.075	9.9
1.080	10.5
1.085	11.2
1.090	11.8
1.095	12.5
1.100	13.2
1.110	14.0

Temperature F°	Correction
54.2	- 0.002
61.5	- 0.001
68	-
73.7	+ 0.001
79.2	+ 0.002
84.3	+ 0.003

The saccharometer is calibrated to work at a temperature of 20°C (68°F). You need to know the temperature of your wort or your wash when taking a measurement. Use your long stem food thermometer to take the temperature. If the wort or wash is higher or lower the 20°C (68°F) use the chart shown above to adjust your reading. Most saccharometers come with this chart.

GRADUATED CYLINDER

The graduated cylinder is a necessary tool for using your hydrometers to measure specific gravity of your mash, wash and distillate. Remember that you are measuring the sugar content of your mash and wash in order to determine their potential alcohol. You are also measuring the abv of your distillate as you distill your wash. Fill the cylinder with fluid from your mash, your wash, or distillate from your still and place the appropriate hydrometer into the cylinder. A turkey baster works good for transferring fluid into the cylinder. Be sure to spin the hydrometer to eliminate any bubbles sticking to it. Just give it a slight spin, let it stop and take your reading. You can get a good graduated cylinder from a brew store or from Amazon.com for about $10.00.

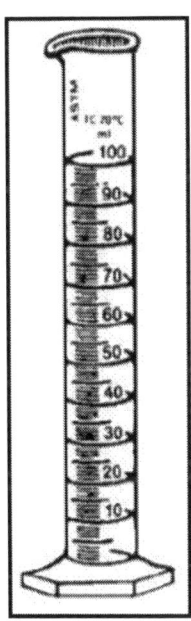
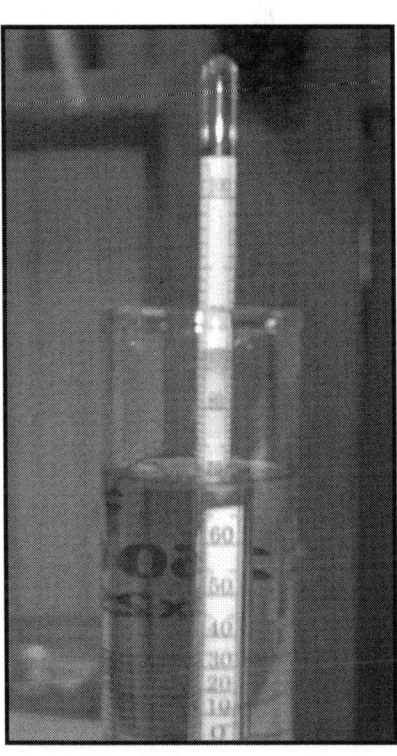

A graduated cylinder makes it easy to take your specific gravity measurements.

Using an alcohol hydrometer to measure abv in a graduated cylinder.

FIFTEEN GALLON COOKING POT WITH LID

The size of your cooking pot will depend on the size of your still and on how big of batches you plan to cook. I recommend a fifteen gallon, triple clad bottom pot. This will allow you to cook batches for a nine gallon (35 liter) still. Get a good quality pot with a triple clad bottom. The thick bottom of a pot like this will help prevent burning your mash on the bottom. A good quality cooking pot can be purchased at a brew store for about $85.00.

FOOD GRADE LONG STEM THERMOMETER

Used to check temperature of mash and distillate. Long stem thermometers are available at brew stores and Amazon.com for $10.00.

LARGE WOODEN STIRRING PADDLE

A nice large stirring paddle makes mash cooking much easier. You can also use large stirring spoons, but if you do, stirring your mash will be a lot more work. You can find a wooden paddle like the one pictured on Amazon.com for $15.00.

PROPANE BURNER FOR COOKING MASH
5 GALLON PROPANE TANK

The Bayou Country Classic propane burner is perfect for cooking large batches of mash. These are available at stores like Walmart, Lowe's, brew stores and like everything, at Amazon.com. They cost about $45.00. Propane tanks are available everywhere. They cost about $45.00.

ELECTRIC HOT PLATE BURNER

You need an electric burner with at least 1500 watts for distilling. If you get one that is less than 1500 watts it will take forever to heat your wash when distilling. A decent burner will cost around $50.00. They are available at most department stores and Amazon.com. Some people use propane burners for distilling. Extra precautions are needed if using an open flame .

EIGHT OUNCE CANNING JARS

You will need around twenty-four 8 ounce canning jars. These will be used during the spirit run. The spirit run is the second distillation you will do on each batch. It is the run where you will be collecting the final product and dividing it into four ounce increments as you distill. This process will be explained in full detail in the distillation chapter. You can get canning jars at any department store for about $8.00 for a case of twelve.

ONE GALLON AGING JARS

Gallon jars are used to collect distillate during your stripping run and can be used to store and age your whiskey. In the chapter on aging we will discuss the jar aging method that is an alternative to aging in oak barrels. I recommend buying four or five of them to start with. You can get them at brew stores for $5.00. They have a shorter style gallon jar at Walmart that will fit underneath your alcohol parrot during your stripping runs.

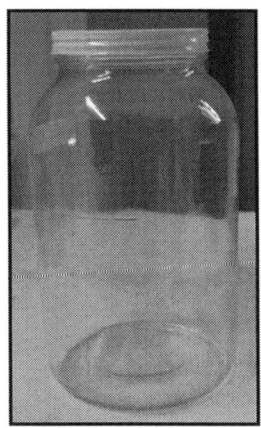

AGING JAR LABELS

It is really important to accurately label your aging jars or things will get mixed up and you won't know what you have in each jar. Photocopy the labels on page 26 and use them for labeling your jars.

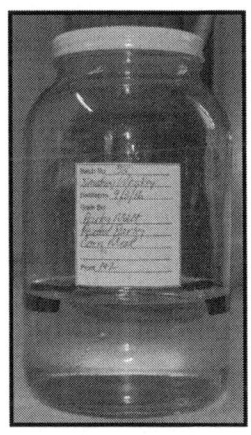

AGING JAR LABELS

```
Batch No._____

Distillation Date_____

Grain Bill
_____
_____
_____
_____

Proof_____
```

```
Batch No._____

Distillation Date_____

Grain Bill
_____
_____
_____
_____

Proof_____
```

Distillation: Date of spirit run.
Grain Bill: Each grain and percentage.
Proof: The aging proof. Normally 125.

DISTILLER'S ACTIVE DRY YEAST (DADY)

DADY is a good all-purpose yeast, in the Saccharomyces cerevisiae species, for whiskey making. This yeast will consistently produce eight to ten percent alcohol depending on the mash grain bill. Yeasts produce various compounds, including esters, during fermentation, that give the distillate different flavors. Once you become a seasoned whiskey maker you could experiment with different yeast strains. I think it's a good idea to start with DADY because it is reliable and far less expensive than other specialty yeast strains. You can buy it from brew stores or from Amazon.com for about $10.00 a pound. This is enough for many batches depending on the size of your still.

YEAST NUTRIENTS

Yeast nutrients need to be added to your mash at the same time that you pitch the yeast. These nutrients are necessary for optimum yeast reproduction and growth. Healthier yeast means better fermentation and more alcohol production. You can buy yeast nutrients at brew stores or at Amazon.com for about $3.00 for a 2 ounce package or about $10.00 for a full pound.

AMYLASE ENZYME

Alpha-amylase enzyme is added to the mash to aid in the saccharification process. The enzyme breaks down starch molecules into single glucose and maltose molecules. Available at brew stores for $3.00. Amylase enzyme can be found at brew stores for about $3.00.

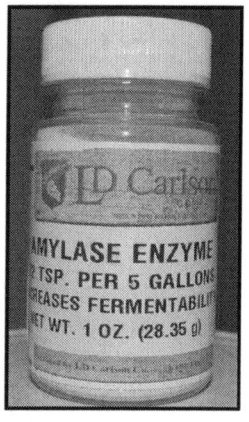

AMERICAN WHITE OAK CUBES

For jar aging you will need either toasted or charred American White Oak cubes. You can buy these at brew stores, but they are very expensive. At about $7.00 for a 2.5 ounce package, you are paying $44.80 for a pound of burnt wood. There are easy ways to produce your own wood cubes to use for aging your whiskey. This process is covered in the next section.

HOMEMADE WHITE OAK AGING CUBES

To make your own charred aging cubes buy some white oak wood, char it with a propane torch or char it on a camp stove. If you want toasted aging cubes, place the wood in your oven at 400°F for about two hours. I cut the pieces up into approximately one inch cubes. The size isn't that important as long as they will fit into your aging jar. You can place the charred or toasted cubes into your gallon jars of newly distilled whiskey, put the lid on and let it age. Three one inch cubes is about the right amount. Leave the wood in until you get the color and flavor you want. You can always experiment with this. Remove the lid once a week to allow volatile vapors to escape. It is best to leave the lid on loosely.

Jar aging, by placing the wood into the whiskey, instead of placing the whiskey into a charred barrel, produces some excellent product in much less time. It takes about six months to produce the best product. Much less than the years it takes in a barrel. This is because you have a much greater surface area of wood per volume of whiskey in a gallon jar than you do in a barrel. We will discuss the aging process in more detail in chapter 3.

Chunks of American White Oak wood

PROPANE TORCH CHARRING

One way to char your wood is to hold the wood with some metal tongs and burn it with your torch. Let it burn until you get a nice yellow flame going, it's good and black, and cracks start to show. When finished, throw in into a bucket of water to cool it off. It's ready to go. Whiskeys are aged with different degrees of charring. Mild, moderate, and heavy are the most common degrees. You can experiment with this. You can buy a propane torch and tongs at most department stores. Propane torches are about $20.00 and metal tongs cost around $5.00.

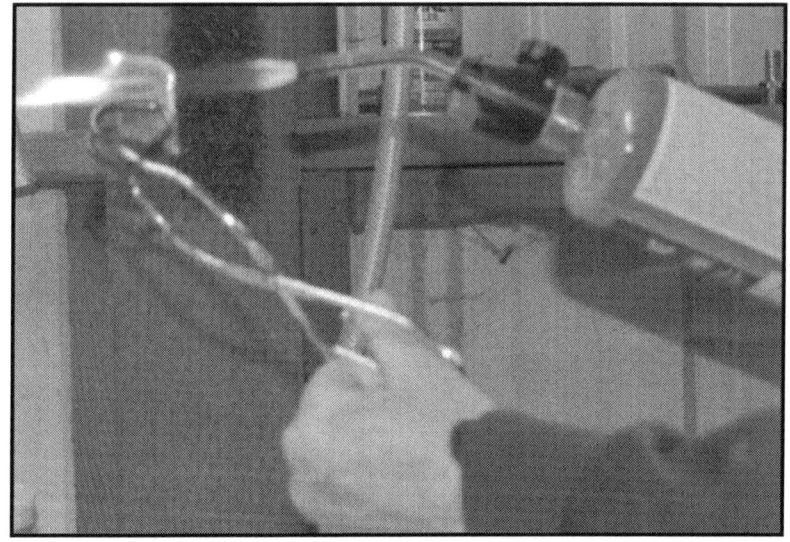

Charred White Oak Cubes

PROPANE CAMP STOVE CHARRING

Using a propane camp stove is the quickest way to char some White Oak wood. Place some chunks on the stove, fire it up and let it burn. You can turn the wood over a few times just like cooking a steak. When they're good and black, and start cracking, they are finished charring. Propane camp stoves are available at camping stores and most department stores. A decent one costs about $40.00.

Some charred White Oak wood. Break these into smaller pieces, say one to three inches long, and place them into your aging jar.

CHARRING TIMES

Number 1 Char: 15 seconds
Number 2 Char: 30 seconds
Number 3 Char: 45 seconds
Number 4 Char: 55 seconds

Number 4 is also known as alligator char, because the charred surface is rough and shiny like alligator skin

12 GALLON FERMENTING BUCKET WITH LID

A 12 gallon fermenting bucket is just the right size to use for a 35 liter still. To use a 35 liter (9 gallon) still you should plan to cook your batches with 8 gallons of water and 24 pounds of grain yielding about a 10 gallon mash. After fermentation you will end up with about 7 gallons of wash. This will fit perfectly into your 35 liter still. You shouldn't fill your still much more than about 3/4 full of wash for distilling. Note: You do not need to use a carboy and pressure valve to ferment your wort. We will discuss this in detail in the fermentation chapter. You can buy a 12 gallon fermentation bucket for about $30.00 at brew stores.

Remember: If you have a still with a different volume than 35 liters, you can just make adjustments to make your wort and wash fit your equipment.

MASH BAG

The mash bag is placed inside your fermenting bucket. After you have cooked your mash, it has cooled to about 24°C (75°F), you have pitched the yeast, mixed it well, and aerated the mash, you pour the mash into the bag. This makes it easy to remove the mash from the fermenting bucket once fermentation is complete. This will be covered in detail in chapter 3. These cost $7.00 at brew stores.

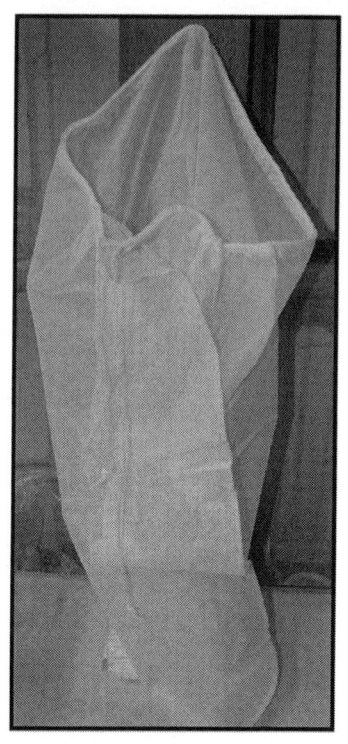

FOOD SCALE

A good food scale is necessary for weighing your grain. You can get one at most department stores for about $40.00.

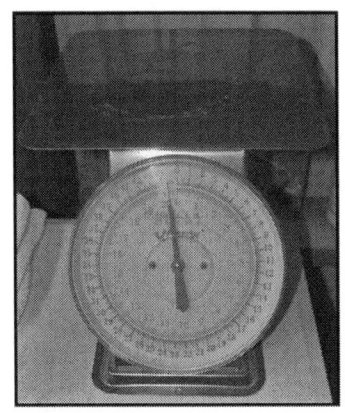

PLASTIC BOWL

A basic plastic salad or mixing bowl works well for measuring and weighing your grain, transferring grain into your cooking pot, transferring mash into your fermentation bucket and for transferring your wash into your still.

KITCHEN STRAINER

A kitchen strainer is useful for taking samples of your wort when checking specific gravity. Place it into the mash pot to separate the wort from the grains.

FLOUR FOR SEALING THE STILL HEAD

You will need to make a flour paste for sealing your still head. The head is removeable and must be sealed when distilling to prevent vapor loss. Mix 1 teaspoon of flour with about 1 teaspoon of water and mix it together. You should end up with a thick paste similar to pancake batter. Spread it around your still head seam with your finger and you are good to go.

Sealing the still head with flour paste.

TURKEY BASTER

Use a turkey baster to draw samples from your wort and your wash. To draw a sample from your mash pot, put your kitchen strainer on top of your mash and draw a sample with your turkey baster. Fill your graduated cylinder, put your saccharometer in and read your SG.

To take a sample from your fermentation bucket, just push the mash bag in on one side and draw a sample. Fill your graduated cylinder and take a reading with your saccharometer.

FERMENTATION CHAMBER

You can ferment your wort in your home, shed, shop, or barn. The requirement is that you need to have a consistent temperature of between 21 and 27°C (70 and 80°F). A fermentation chamber is convenient and easy to build. The one shown below is made of plywood. It is 4 feet wide, 2 feet deep and 4 feet high. Line the inside walls and door with 1 inch thick insulation panels. The door latches shut and the temperature is controlled with a small space heater with a thermostat. It works great and you can fit 2 fermentation buckets inside. You can get the insulation panels at Lowe's or Home Depot for a couple of bucks each.

HOME MADE MASH PRESS

The Home Made Mash Press is inexpensive, easy to use, and quite effective. You will need a 16 gallon plastic tub, a 2X4 foot piece of plastic bench top or similar material, and a thick piece of plywood large enough to cover your mash bag. Set up your press like the one shown below. Stand on the plywood and your weight will press out the wort. You can slowly rock back and forth to squeeze out every last drop. Plastic tubs are available to feed stores for about $20. You can get the bench top from Southwest Agriplastics for about $20. Website: swapinc.com

16 Gallon plastic tub

Greenhouse bench top

Home Made Mash Press
The mash bag is placed between the plywood and the greenhouse bench top.

WORT CHILLER

A wort chiller is optional, but it is a nice piece of equipment to have. After your mash has been cooked and rested for 90 minutes you need to cool it down to 24 to 27°C (75 to 80°F) before pitching your yeast. A good wort chiller can chill your wort down to yeast pitching temperature in 15 to 30 minutes depending on the volume of your mash. Another option is to place your cooking pot into a large barrel or sink full of cold water.

Fifty foot stainless steel wort chiller. Buy these at brew stores, on-line stores, Amazon.com. Cost $35 to $100 depending on quality.

PH METER

Used to check the pH of your mash and your wort. You can use pH test strips, but a meter will give you more accurate readings. Buy these at brew stores or on-line. Cost about $25.00.

DUCT TAPE

You will need duct tape for recording your temperature and abv as you distill using the 24 pint sized canning jars. Place a line of duct tape on the edge of a table as shown below. As you fill your small jars half full during distillation, you will place them on the table and record the vapor temperature and abv. This example shows the temperature in Celsius. Some stills have a Celsius vapor thermometer and some have Fahrenheit. You will be reading the abv from the alcohol hydrometer placed in your parrot. Notice how the vapor temperature goes up and the abv goes down as you continue the distilling run.

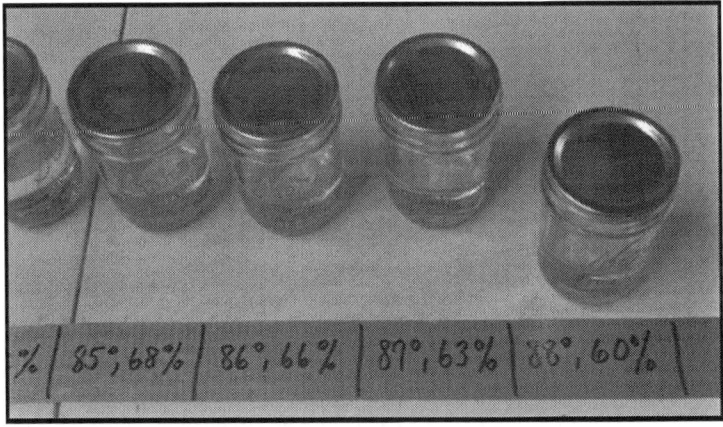

You will also need to record the batch number and date on your fermentation bucket. Duct tape works well for that also.

PRODUCT RECORD

Keeping good records of each batch you make is EXTREMELY important. You need accurate data of each batch so that you can make improvements in your process and in case you want to duplicate a certain batch that you really like. I recommend using a three ring notebook and a product record sheet like the one shown below. This is a 2 page record. It is also set up as a step by step instruction sheet. Follow the steps and record your data as you go. Both pages are shown on pages 43 and 44. You should photocopy these and use them.

PRODUCT RECORD

Batch Number: 43 Name: Bourbon

Grain Bill
Corn Meal - 60%, 14.4 lbs. 1t Amylase Enzyme
Rye - 25%, 6.0 lbs. 5t Yeast Nutrient
Barley Malt - 15%, 3.6 lbs. 5t DADY
24 lbs.

Mash
Date 10/30/16 Time 12:00 PM Water Qty. 8 gal. Total Mash Vol. 10 gal.
Heat water to 167°F. Gelatinize corn, 158 - 167°F, 60 minutes. 162°F, 1:45 - 2:45 PM
Heat mash back to 158°F. Add other grains, amylase enzyme, rest at 148°F for 90 minutes ✓
Chill to 75 - 80°F. ✓ Specific gravity 1.071 Potential Alcohol 9.5 %

Pitch Yeast
Date 10/30/16 Time 5:00 PM Mash temp. 80°F
Yeast Type DADY Qty 5t Yeast nutrients ✓ Qty 5t
Stir, aerate - pour between 5 gallon buckets 3 times. Pour into fermentation bucket ✓

Fermentation On the grain.
Ferment at 70 - 80F. About 3 days.
Stop when final specific gravity reaches 1.001.
Start Date 10/30/16 Time 5:30 PM Starting SG 1.071 Starting PA 9.5 %
End Date 11/3/16 Time 3:00 PM Ending SG 1.004 Ending PA 1.5 %

Stripping Run Net PA 8.0 %
Heat slowly. Keep heat low, 80 - 82C. Run to 96C or 10% abv. 8 Hours. Low Wines.
Date 11/4/16 Start Time 9:30 AM End Time 8:00 PM Distillate Temp 60°F
1st Drips: Time 11:30 AM Temp 55°C Fast Drips: Time 12:00 PM Temp 70°C
Start abv 74 % End abv 16 % Final Blended abv 42 % Qty 166 oz.
Temp. 85°C Temp. 96°C

42

PRODUCT RECORD

Batch Number_____ **Name**_____

Grain Bill
_____
_____
_____

Mash
Date_____ Time_____ Water Qty_____ Total Mash Vol._____

Heat water to 167°F. Gelatinize corn, 158 - 167°F, 60 minutes.

Heat mash back to 158°F. Add other grains, amylase enzyme, rest at 148°F for 90 minutes. Chill to 75 - 80°F _____
Record Specific Gravity_____ Potential Alcohol_____

Pitch Yeast
Date _____ Time_____ Mash temp._____

Yeast Type_____ Qty_____ Yeast nutrients_____ Qty _____

Stir, aerate - pour between 5 gallon buckets 3 times. Pour into fermentation bucket _____

Fermentation
Ferment at 70 - 80°F. About 3 days. Stop when final sg reaches 1.01.
Start Date_____ Time_____ Starting SG_____ Starting PA _____

End Date _____ Time_____ Ending SG_____ Ending PA _____
                                                   Net PA_____

Stripping Run
Heat slowly. Run to 96°C or 10% abv. Approx. 8 Hours. Low Wines.

Date_____ Start Time_____ End Time_____

Distillate Temp_____ 1st Drips: Time_____ Temp_____

Fast Drips: Time_____ Temp_____

Start abv_____ Temp_____

End abv_____ Temp_____

Final Blended abv _____ Qty_____

Batch Number_____ Name_____

Spirit Run
Use 24, 8 oz. jars. Fill half full. Heat slowly. Takes about 3 hours.

Date_____ Start Time_____ End Time_____ Added Water Qty____

Distillate Temp_____ Dump first 8 ounce jar (methanol) _____

1st Drips: Time_____   Temp_____

Fast Drips: Time_____   Temp_____

Jar Data and Cuts (Temp and abv) Use 75% abv - 65% abv cuts for highest quality. Record temp and abv for each 4 oz. jar.

1_____	2_____	3_____	4_____	5_____	6_____
7_____	8_____	9_____	10_____	11_____	12_____
13_____	14_____	15_____	16_____	17_____	18_____
19_____	20_____	21_____	22_____	23_____	24_____

Heads Cut: ABV_____   Temp_____   Tails Cut: ABV_____

Temp_____   Total Qty_____   Finish ABV_____

Aging
Qty_____   ABV_____   Proof_____

Beginning Date_____   Ending Date_____

Toasted White Oak Cubes_____
Charred White Oak Cubes_____

Age at 125 proof, 62.5% abv. Age for 6 months for best product. Proof down (dilute) to drinking proof after aging. Use filtered water.

Proofing Down
Water Added_____   Final ABV_____   Final Proof_____

Filtering and Bottling Date_____   Total Final Qty_____

Use coffee filter for whiskey, carbon filter for vodka.

Final Notes
_____
_____
_____

MISCELLANEOUS SUPPLIES

SPACE HEATER WITH THERMOSTAT
A small space heater with a thermostat makes it easy to control the temperature in your fermentation chamber.

5 GALLON BUCKETS WITH HANDLES
You will need two 5 gallon buckets for aerating your mash and transferring your fermented wash into your still.

STORAGE TUB WITH LID
A plastic tub works great for storing your supplies like hydrometers and other small items.

PLASTIC GARBAGE CAN WITH LID
A large garbage can is necessary to store your grains in. Keeps the mice away.

PLASTIC FUNNEL
A plastic funnel is used to pour your whiskey into bottles.

SHOP RAGS
Shop rags will be used throughout the whiskey making process. It's a good idea to have a few on hand for every batch you make.

ROPE
You will need about 6 feet of 3/8" rope to tie your mash bag to a 4X4 beam so it can drain once fermentation is complete.

4X4 WOOD POST
An 8 foot 4X4 works well for tying your mash bag up to for drainage.

METAL FOOD TONGS
Food tongs are used to hold pieces of white oak wood while they are being charred with a propane torch.

GREENHOUSE BENCH TOP
Used to press out wort from the mash. Southwest Agriplastics Inc., swapinc.com. About $20.00.

SHARPIE
Use a sharpie to record your temperature and abv when distilling and for labeling your fermentation buckets when fermenting.

COFFEE FILTERS
Coffee filters are used to filter your whiskey when the aging process is complete.

ACTIVATED CARBON FILTER (FOR VODKA)
Vodka is normally filtered through activated carbon to remove as many congeners as possible. Available at brew stores.

16 OUNCE MEASURING CUP (CLEAR)
You will need a measuring cup to measure the quantity of your distillate.

CLEANING STATION, HOSE
A wood bench, hose and running water are nice to have for cleaning and rinsing your equipment.

BLEACH
Bleach is used to sanitize your tools, 5 gallon buckets and fermentation buckets. Do not use bleach on any cooper equipment, it will corrode it.

WHITE VINEGAR
Vinegar works well for cleaning your still, alcohol parrot and anything made of copper. Pour about 2 cups into your still, add a gallon of water, scrub out the still and rinse with water 3 times.

SCRUBBER PADS OR SCRUBBER BRUSH
Scrubber pads or a scrubber brush will work well for cleaning your still and other equipment.

SIXTEEN GALLON TUB
Used to make a home made mash press. Available at livestock feed stores. About $15.00.

CHAPTER 3

Making Whiskey

You've read the first two chapters and you have all the necessary supplies and equipment - it's time to make whiskey! We will examine an example batch and look at each step of the process in detail. *

THE GRAIN BILL

The grain bill is simply a list of the grains you are going to use to make your whiskey. For our example batch we will choose a standard bourbon grain bill and we'll use that example to show you each step in the whiskey making process. **Everything we do will be calculated for a 35 liter (9 gallon) still.** This is a nice sized still. It is easy to work with and will produce three to four fifths of final product per batch. If you have a different sized still it is easy to modify the grain bill based on the 35 liter still quantities. Be sure to read through the example batch first, then you will be prepared to make any of the other recipes that follow.

Whiskey grain bills normally have from 2 to 3 lbs. of grain per gallon of water. I find that using 3 lbs. of grain per gallon of water works well. For our example batch we will use 8 gallons of water and 24 lbs. of grain, (3 X 8 = 24 lbs. of grain). This will produce about 10 gallons of mash due to the added volume of the grain. The actual volume will vary depending on your grain bill. Follow the cooking instructions in this chapter carefully! The amount of actual wash going into the still after fermentation will be about 7 gallons, just right for a 9 gallon still. Remember that you shouldn't fill your still much more than about three fourths full.

Note: There is a summarized list of the whiskey making steps in appendix B.

EXAMPLE BOURBON GRAIN BILL AND RECIPE

For our whiskey production example we will use the following grain bill and recipe. After studying this information you will be able to modify the amounts for your particular still size.

Water - 8 gal. (10 gal. total mash volume - explained below)
Corn Meal 60%, .6 X 24 = 14.4 lbs.
Rye 25%, .25 X 24 = 6.0 lbs.
Barley Malt 15%, .15 X 24 = 3.6 lbs.
Amylase Enzyme - 1 teaspoon (1/2 t per 5 gal. mash)
Yeast Nutrient - 5 teaspoons (1/2 t per gal. mash)
Distiller's Active Dry Yeast - 5 teaspoons (1/2 t per gal. mash)

Note: In chapter 4 you will find 16 more grain bills and recipes.

HOW TO CALCULATE THE TOTAL MASH VOLUME

9 Gallon Still Example

To determine the amount of water needed figure about 90% of your still size.

.9 X 9 = 8.1 gallons of water (round off to 8 gal.)

The actual volume of mash will come out a little more than the amount of water you use. This is because the grains will add some volume to the total mash quantity. You can estimate the added volume from the grain by multiplying **.08** times the number of pounds of grain and adding it to the gallons of water. .08 is the estimated amount, in gallons, that one pound of grain will add to the total mash volume. The reason the grain adds only a fractional amount to the total mash volume is due to the porosity of the grain particles, or the air space between the particles. This space fills with water. The grain also absorbs some of the water as well. This number (.08) is an <u>estimate</u>. It will vary somewhat depending on the particular grain bill you are using.

8 gal. water X 3 lbs. grain = 24 lbs. grain needed

24 X .08 = 1.92 gal. added volume from grain (round off to 2 gal.)

8 + 2 = 10 gal. total mash volume

The question is, will the wash from this batch fit into your still? Remember, you don't want to fill your still more the 3/4 full. You will typically get about 70% of your total mash volume returned as wash.

10 gal. mash X .70 (percentage of wash recovered from mash) = 7.0 gal. wash

7/9 = .78

This wash will fill 78% of your still. Very close to 3/4 (75%) limit. The 10 gallon mash will work.

The math calculations can help you meet the volume limits of your still. You don't need to meet those figures exactly. They are just guidelines. When cooking batches for your own still you will need to experiment and make adjustments as necessary. "Learn by doing," as they say.

BASIC STRUCTURE OF THE WHISKEY RECIPES

Using this information you can determine the quantities to use for your particular still size.

Grain Bill - 3 lbs. of grain per gallon of water.
Amylase Enzyme - 1/2 teaspoon per 5 gallons of mash
Yeast Nutrient - 1/2 teaspoon per gallon of mash
Distiller's Active Dry Yeast - 1/2 teaspoon per gallon of mash
Yogurt (Optional) - 1 teaspoon per gallon of mash

HOW TO CALCULATE YOUR GRAIN QUANTITIES

BASIC STRAIGHT BOURBON

<u>9 Gallon still example</u>

8 Gallons of water
24 Pounds of grain (8 gal. water X 3 lbs. grain = 24 lbs. grain needed)
10 Gallon mash

Just multiply the percentage of each kind of grain in your grain bill by the total amount of grain required.

Corn Meal   60%,   .6 X 24 = 14.4 lbs.
Rye   25%,   .25 X 24 = 6.0 lbs.
Barley Malt 15%,   .15 X 24 = 3.6 lbs.
Amylase Enzyme 1 t (1/2 teaspoon per 5 gallons mash)
Yeast Nutrient 5 t (1/2 teaspoon per gallon mash)
DADY 5 t (1/2 teaspoon per gallon mash)
Yogurt (optional) 10 t (1 teaspoon per gallon mash) - some distillers use yogurt as a source of Lactobacillus bacteria.

NOTE: You may notice different grain bills for Straight Bourbon. As long as they contain at least 51% corn and the rest of the grain bill contains rye and barley, it is considered Bourbon.

THE MASH

WE WILL USE THE EXAMPLE BOURBON GRAIN BILL AND RECIPE FROM PAGE 48. YOU CAN USE THIS PROCESS FOR ANY RECIPE.

When making whiskey and other spirits the first step is to cook the mash. The mash consists of water, grains, and enzymes added to help in the saccharification process.

Start by filling your mash cooking pot with the required amount of water for your batch. Heat the water to 75°C (167°). If your grain bill includes corn, mix that in first and let it gelatinize for one hour. This helps break the bonds between the starch molecules in the corn and allows the corn to absorb more water. The mixture will become very thick as it gelatinizes. It will become thin again after the other grains and enzymes are added. Keep the temperature between 70 and 75°C (158 and 167°F). After one hour, heat your mash back to 70°C (158°F). Add the other grains included in your grain bill. Mix well to prevent clumping. Add amylase enzyme and mix again. Your mash temperature will drop down to about 64°C (148°F). Keep the temperature here and let the mash rest for 90 minutes. Be sure to put the lid on the pot. You may need to wrap a blanket around your pot to keep the temperature from dropping. If you have a high quality heavy duty cooking pot you probably won't need the blanket. You can always add more heat with your burner if necessary. After 90 minutes have passed you will need to chill your mash down to about 24°C (75°F). You can do this be using a wort chiller or place your cooking pot into a large tub of cold water. An alternative method is to let your mash rest overnight. It will be cooled down by the next morning. After cooling down check the specific gravity (SG) of your wort with a saccharometer (sugar hydrometer). This will show you the sugar content of your wort and allow you to determine the potential alcohol. SG should be somewhere around 1.08 which corresponds with a potential alcohol of 10.5%. Record the SG and potential alcohol in your distilling record.

STEPS FOR COOKING THE MASH

STEP 1: PUT 8 GALLONS OF WATER INTO YOUR COOKING POT

STEP 2: HEAT THE WATER TO 75°C (167°F).

STEP 3: ADD THE CORN MEAL AND GELATINIZE

For any grain bill that includes corn, the corn must be gelatinized. Put in 14.4 lbs. of corn meal. Stir constantly as you add the corn or you will get corn dough balls that are hard to mix in. Once it is well mixed, put the lid on the pot and let it sit for one hour. You want to keep the temperature between 70°C (158°F) and 75°C (167°F). The corn mash will get very thick. It will liquefy after you mix in the barley malt and amylase enzyme later on.

Mix the corn in thoroughly. A couple of minutes of stirring will do the job.

Put the lid on and let rest for one hour.

STEP 4: ADD THE REMAINING GRAINS

Heat the mash back to 70°C (158°F).
Add 6 lbs. of rye, stir it into the mash.
Add 3.6 lbs. of barley malt, stir it into the mash.
Once you mix in the other grains the temperature will drop to approximately 148°F, this is where you want to be. Add some heat if necessary.

STEP 5: ADD THE AMYLASE ENZYME

Amylase enzyme is added at the rate of 1/2 teaspoon per 5 gallons of mash. For this batch of 10 gallons add 1 teaspoon. Mix everything together well. A few minutes of good mixing will do.

STEP 6: CHECK THE pH OF YOUR MASH

pH stands for potential hydrogen. pH measures the acidity and alkalinity of a substance. We are concerned about the pH of our mash, and our wort prior to fermentation. The pH scale is a logarithmic scale that goes from 0 to 14. Seven is neutral, anything below 7 is acidic, and anything above 7 is alkaline. Acidic substances have a high concentration of hydrogen ions (H^+) and alkaline substances have a high concentration of hydroxyl ions (OH^-).

In the distilling business the optimum pH for mash is between 5.2 and 5.7, moderately acidic. This pH range improves the activity of the enzymes responsible for saccharification and gives us a better conversion of the starches in the mash to glucose. It is a good idea to check the pH of your mash with a pH test strip or a digital pH meter. The good news is that mash can naturally be in the pH range of 5.2 to 5.7 because grains are acidic by nature. But, this is not always the case depending on the particular grain bill you are cooking. The water you are using or the particular grains you are using can often produce a pH value that is above the optimum range. You can easily lower the pH by adding citric acid, lactic acid, gypsum, phosphoric acid, lemon juice, or 5.2 pH Stabilizer to your mash. Add 1 teaspoon at a time, mix it in, then recheck your pH. If you have a pH that is too low, you can add lime (calcium carbonate) or baking soda (sodium bicarbonate) to your mash. This will raise the pH.

STEP 7: REST THE MASH FOR 90 MINUTES

Place the lid on your pot and let the mash rest for 90 minutes. You only need to keep the temperature at 64°C (148°F) for 90 minutes. This is where saccharification is occurring.

STEP 8: COOL THE MASH

Next, we need to cool the mash down to about 24°C (75°F). You can use a wort chiller after 90 minutes or you can let the mash rest overnight, but it is best to cool the mash quickly. The goal is to allow the temperature to drop down to around 24°C (75°F). If you're going to leave it overnight just bring it to 64°C (148°F) then let it rest until the next morning. When the temperature drops to about 24°C (75°F) you can pitch your yeast.

 Wort chiller

STEP 9: CHECK THE SPECIFIC GRAVITY OF THE WORT

Once the wort has cooled to between 24 and 27°C (75 and 80°F), place your kitchen strainer into the mash bucket to separate some wort from the grain. Using your turkey baster draw some wort and place it into your graduated cylinder. Fill it to within about 3 inches of the top. Use your saccharometer to check the specific gravity of the wort. It should read somewhere around 1.080 which equates to a potential alcohol of 10.5%. Your actual SG could be a little less or a little more. Your potential alcohol should be between 8 and 12%. Every batch will vary by a small amount. Not to worry. Record your SG and PA in your distillation record.

Drawing out some wort using a kitchen strainer and turkey baster.

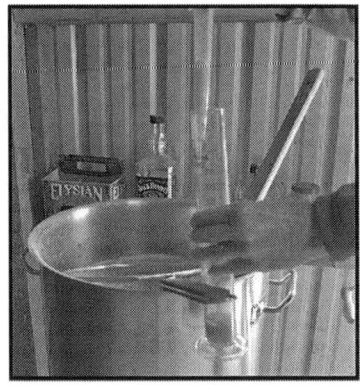

Placing the wort into the graduated cylinder.

Placing the saccharometer into the graduated cylinder and reading the SG.

FERMENTATION

Fermentation is the process of converting sugars, like glucose and maltose, into acids, carbon dioxide (CO_2) and various alcohols by yeasts. Putting yeast into the mash or the wort, so they can consume glucose and produce alcohol, is called pitching the yeast. The alcohol we are primarily interested in is ethanol (2 C_2H_5OH). During both respiration and fermentation yeast cells break down glucose molecules to release energy. This is called glycolysis. The breakdown of glucose also releases carbon atoms which can be used by the yeast to grow and reproduce (budding). There are two primary methods of fermentation used in distilling alcohol, **fermenting on the grain** and **fermenting off the grain**. Grain bills that contain corn are usually fermented on the grain because corn is more difficult to sparge than all grain whiskeys. Bourbon and Tennessee whiskeys are normally fermented on the grain, while single malt whiskeys and Irish whiskeys are normally fermented off the grain. Some believe that fermenting on the grain produces a more flavorful spirit. We will explain both methods.

FERMENTING ON THE GRAIN

Fermenting on the grain involves placing yeast directly into the cooled mash for fermentation.

STEP 1: CHECK THE pH OF YOUR MASH

Before you pitch your yeast and start fermentation you should check your mash pH again. Yeast do best when the pH of your mash is moderately acidic. The best pH range is from 4.0 to 4.5. This pH range keeps the yeast healthy and helps control undesirable bacterial growth. You can easily lower the pH by adding citric acid, lactic acid, gypsum, phosphoric acid, lemon juice, or 5.2 pH Stabilizer to your mash. Add 1 teaspoon at a time, mix it in, then recheck your pH. If you have a pH that is too low, you can add lime (calcium carbonate) or baking soda (sodium bicarbonate) to your mash. This will raise the pH.

STEP 2: SANITIZE YOUR BUCKETS, MASH BAG PLASTIC BOWL, FERMENTATION BUCKET AND LID

Pour about 1 tablespoon of bleach into one of your 5 gallon buckets. Add a couple of gallons of water. Use that to wash out your other 5 gallon bucket, your mash bag, your plastic salad bowl and your fermentation bucket and lid. Rinse off everything with running water. I recommend doing this outside of your building with a hose. Use the triple rinse method. That is, rinse everything off or out three times.

STEP 3: PLACE YOUR MASH BAG INTO THE FERMENTATION BUCKET AND TIE IT IN PLACE

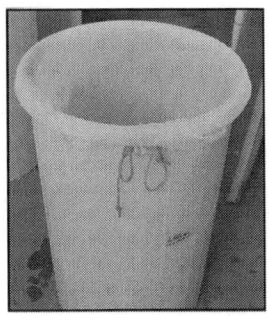

STEP 4: ADD YEAST NUTRIENTS

The source of energy consumed by yeast is glucose, but yeast also requires other nutrients in order to reproduce and grow. Yeast nutrient blends contain a mix of trace elements, inorganic nitrogen, organic nitrogen, zinc and phosphates that helps yeast grow and complete fermentation. Yeast nutrients are added to the mash at the same time as the yeast is pitched. You need 1/2 teaspoon of yeast nutrients per gallon of mash. Put 5 teaspoons of yeast nutrient into your mash pot. Mix it in well.

STEP 5: PITCH THE YEAST

The next step is to add yeast, otherwise known as pitching the yeast. The yeast nutrients provide essential nitrogen and minerals to the yeast to help them grow and reproduce. Yeasts are in the species Saccharomyces cerevisise. There are many different strains within that species. A good yeast to start out with is Distiller's Active Dry Yeast or DADY. It is a general purpose distilling yeast that will do a good job fermenting the wort.

You will use 1/2 teaspoon of yeast per gallon of mash. Get your yeast from the refrigerator, place 5 teaspoons in a small plastic bag or bowl and let it warm to room temperature for about 15 minutes. You don't want to pitch cold yeast into a batch of warm wort, the quick temperature change could kill the yeast. Mix the yeast in well.

Pitching the yeast

STEP 6: AERATE THE MASH

After mixing, the mash should be aerated by pouring it back and forth between two five gallon buckets three times. This introduces more oxygen into the mash for the yeast to utilize.

Remove the mash using your plastic bowl. It is much easier to do it with a bowl in small amounts rather than trying to lift and pour your whole cooking pot. Pour bowls of mash into a 5 gallon bucket until the bucket is about half full. Next pour the mash between your two five gallon buckets three times. This will aerate the mash. After aerating pour the half bucket into your fermentation bucket. Keep doing this until the mash pot is empty and all of the mash is in your fermentation bucket.

Pouring mash from the cooking pot into a 5 gallon bucket.

Aerating the mash by pouring between two buckets three times.

STEP 7: POUR THE MASH INTO YOUR FERMENTATION BUCKET

After aerating, tie a mash bag into a fermentation bucket and pour the mash into the bucket.

Using the 10 gallon mash recipe, as we are for this example batch, will end up filling your fermentation bucket up to about 4 inches from the top. The grain cap will rise almost to the top of the bucket. This is perfect and maximizes production for the size of your equipment.

STEP 8: PUT THE LID ON YOUR FERMENTATION BUCKET AND LABEL IT

Include batch number and date

STEP 9: PUT THE FERMENTATION BUCKET INTO YOUR FERMENTATION CHAMBER

Set your heater at 24 to 27°C (75 to 80°F) and close the door. Fermentation has begun.

PROCEDURES DURING FERMENTATION

CHECK FOR THE GRAIN CAP AND CRACKLING SOUND

Check your batch after the first 2 to 3 hours. Pull the lid off of the fermenting bucket. You should see the grain cap. When the yeast really start growing and producing CO_2, a grain cap will form at the top of the fermentation bucket. This is a good sign because it shows that the yeast are actively fermenting. You should also be able to hear a distinct crackling sound, like Rice Krispies in a bowl of milk. That is the sound of the CO_2 bubbling up to the surface.

Grain Cap

Grain Cap

CHECK TEMPERATURE OF YOUR FERMENTATION CHAMBER

Check the temperature of your fermentation chamber each day. You want it to stay around 24° to 27°C (75° to 80°F).

CHECK THE SG OF THE WASH

Fermentation should be complete in about 3 or 4 days. After 3 days take a SG reading with your saccharometer. When the SG drops to 1.010 fermentation is complete.

When your SG is at 1.010 or close to it, all or most of the glucose has been converted to alcohol and the yeast are dying off. You will not the hear the crackling sound any longer and the grain cap may have sunk back into the wash. Dead yeast will be building up on the bottom of your fermenter. Fermentation is complete at this point. It's time to pull the mash bag and recover the wash.

Remove the lid off of your fermentation bucket. Pull the mash bag in a few inches in order to separate the wash from the grain. Draw wash out using your turkey baster and fill your graduated cylinder up to about 3 inches from the top.

Filling the graduated cylinder with wash.

Checking the SG of the wash with a saccharometer. If it's at 1.010 or close to it fermentation is complete.

RECOVERING THE WASH

The wort, which was the liquid with the mash, has been fermented and is now called the wash. It will normally contain between 8 and 10% alcohol. Our task now is to separate the wash from the grain and prepare for distillation.

STEP 1: OPEN YOUR FERMENTATION BUCKET AND TIE A ROPE AROUND THE TOP PART OF THE MASH BAG

STEP 2: PULL THE BUCKET UNDERNEATH A SOLID 4X4 BEAM.

STEP 3: PULL THE MASH BAG UP AND TIE IT TO THE 4X4 BEAM AND LET IT DRAIN

Put the rope over the top of the 4 X 4 and slowly pull the mash bag up so that the wash can drain back into the fermentation bucket. Wind the rope around the 4 X 4 several times and tie it off so the bag will not slip back into the bucket. You can let it drain overnight or you can squeeze the liquid out of the mash bag. When it is finished draining you will end up with about 7 gallons of wash in your fermentation bucket. After it settles you will see about an inch layer of dead yeast in the bottom, this is called the lees. You can dump the lees or leave them in the wash when you distill. Some believe the lees add flavor to the distillate. It's a personal choice.

4X4 support beam laying across the corner of a rail fence. This is a good setup for hanging your mash bag to drain out the wash before distillation.

Mash bag tied to a 4 X 4 on top. This allows the wash to drain from the mash bag into the fermentation bucket.

You can speed up the process by squeezing the mash with your hands.

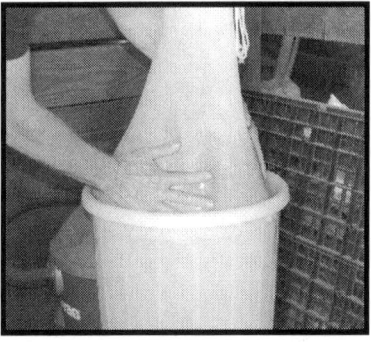

STEP 4: PRESS OUT THE REMAINING WASH

There are many ways to squeeze out the last bit of wash, you can't get it all with your hands. I like the home made press shown below, it works really well. You place a piece of greenhouse bench top or similar material on top of a large plastic tub. Next, place your mash bag on top of the bench top. Then place a piece of plywood on top of the bag and stand on it. Your weight will squeeze out the remaining wash. Now you are ready for the stripping run, page 74.

16 Gallon plastic tub

Greenhouse bench top

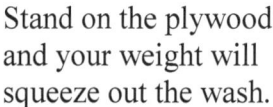

Stand on the plywood and your weight will squeeze out the wash.

FERMENTING OFF THE GRAIN

When fermenting off the grain, the wort is removed from the mash prior to fermentation. *If you ferment on the grain you can skip this part and go directly to the stripping run, page 74.*

STEP 1: COOL THE MASH

You need to cool your mash first. This can be accomplished by using a mash chiller or you can simply put the pot into a large tub of cold water. You can also let the mash sit and cool overnight, just be sure to keep the lid on to prevent anything from getting into the pot. You should cool your mash down to between 24° and 27°C (75° - 80°F).

STEP 2: SANITIZE ALL OF YOUR EQUIPMENT

Pour about 1 tablespoon of bleach into one of your 5 gallon buckets. Add a couple of gallons of water. Use that to wash out your other 5 gallon bucket, your mash bag, your plastic salad bowl and your fermentation bucket and lid. Rinse off everything with running water. I recommend doing this outside of your building with a hose. Use the triple rinse method. That is, rinse everything off or out three times.

STEP 3: SEPARATE THE WORT FROM THE MASH

Separating the wort from the mash is called lautering. After cooling, pour the mash into a mash bag which is inside of your fermentation bucket. Pull the bag out of the bucket and hang it on your 4X4 beam so it can drain into a bucket or tub. The mash bag can be hand squeezed and pressed with a mash press to remove the last bit of wort. See the home made mash press on page 68.

STEP 4: TIE THE MASH BAG UP TO YOUR 4X4 BEAM

Allow the wort to drain out of the bag. You can speed up the process by squeezing the mash with your hands.

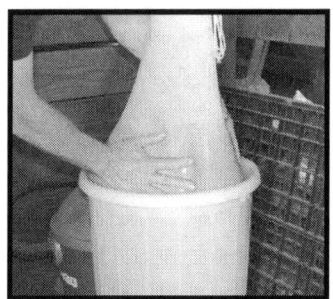

STEP 5: PRESS OUT THE REMAINING WORT

There are many ways to squeeze out the last bit of wort from your mash, you can't get it all with your hands. I like the home made mash press shown on pages 39 and 68, it works really well.

STEP 6: SPARGE THE MASH (OPTIONAL)

Sparging involves trickling hot water over the drained mash in order to extract more sugar from the grain. Sparging is certainly not required, but it can increase the volume of fermentable wort. It is the normal procedure when making whiskey's with all barley mash. These include single malt whiskey (Scotch style) and Irish whiskey. Grain bills which include corn are more difficult to sparge due to the gelatinous nature of corn when heated in water. If you decide to sparge your mash after draining the initial wort you can purchase a mash tun with a false bottom that allows added water to be filtered through the mash or you can use less expensive methods. A method I have found to be effective is to sprinkle hot water over the grain while it is still in the mash bag. Sprinkling is important because you don't want a large stream of water to make a channel down through the grain. You want an even distribution of water over the grain bed so that it will slowly soak down through the grain.

After draining and pressing the wort from your mash with the mash press, heat 1 pint of water per gallon of water used to make the mash, to 77°C (170°F). For example, if you started your mash with 8 gallons of water, you would use 8 pints or 1 gallon for your sparge water. You must limit the amount of sparge water you use or you will end up with a larger than desired quantity of wort. This will end up producing excess wash that may not fit in your still.

Use a watering can to slowly sprinkle the water over the grain. Let it drain and then press out the remaining liquid with your mash press. Add this to the rest of your wort.

STEP 7: POUR ALL OF THE WORT INTO YOUR FERMENTATION BUCKET

STEP 8: CHECK THE SPECIFIC GRAVITY OF THE WORT

Be sure to check the SG of your wort after combining the

sparge water with the rest of your wort. It will have dropped down some due to the lower SG of the sparge water you are adding. Record this in your product record.

STEP 9: CHECK THE pH OF YOUR WORT

Before you pitch your yeast and start fermentation you should check your wort pH. Yeast do best when the pH of your wort is moderately acidic. The best pH range is from 4.0 to 4.5. This pH range keeps the yeast healthy and helps control undesirable bacterial growth. You can easily lower the pH by adding citric acid, lactic acid, gypsum, phosphoric acid, lemon juice, or 5.2 pH Stabilizer to your mash. Add 1 teaspoon at a time, mix it in, then recheck your pH. If you have a pH that is too low, you can add lime (calcium carbonate) or baking soda (sodium bicarbonate) to your mash. This will raise the pH.

STEP 10: ADD THE YEAST NUTRIENTS

The source of energy consumed by yeast is glucose, but yeast also requires other nutrients in order to reproduce and grow. Yeast nutrient blends contain a mix of trace elements, inorganic nitrogen, organic nitrogen, zinc and phosphates that helps yeast grow and complete fermentation. Yeast nutrients are added to the mash at the same time as the yeast is pitched. You need 1/2 teaspoon of yeast nutrients per gallon of mash. Put 5 teaspoons of yeast nutrient into your mash pot. Mix it in well.

STEP 11: PITCH THE YEAST - MIX WELL

The next step is to add yeast, otherwise known as pitching the yeast. The yeast nutrients provide essential nitrogen and minerals to the yeast to help them grow and reproduce. Yeasts are in the species Saccharomyces cerevisise. There are many different strains within that species. A good yeast to start out with is Distiller's Active Dry Yeast or DADY. It is a general purpose distilling yeast that will do a good job fermenting the wort.

You will use 1/2 teaspoon of yeast per gallon of mash. Get your yeast from the refrigerator, place 5 teaspoons in a small plastic bag or bowl and let it warm to room temperature for about 15 minutes. You don't want to pitch cold yeast into a batch of warm wort, the quick temperature change could kill the yeast. Mix the yeast in well.

STEP 12: AERATE THE WORT

After mixing, the wort should be aerated by pouring it back and forth between two five gallon buckets three times. This introduces more oxygen into the mash for the yeast to utilize.
Remove the wort using your plastic bowl. Pour bowls of wort into a 5 gallon bucket until the bucket is about half full. Next pour the wort between your two five gallon buckets three times. This will aerate the wort. After aerating pour the half bucket into your fermentation bucket. Keep doing this until the all of the wort has been aerated.

STEP 13: PLACE THE FERMENTATION BUCKET INTO THE FERMENTATION CHAMBER

PROCEDURES DURING FERMENTATION

CHECK FOR THE FIZZING SOUND
This should occur about three hours after pitching the yeast as carbon dioxide is being released. You should also see the kraeusen forming on top of the wort.

CHECK THE TEMPERATURE OF YOUR FERMENTATION CHAMBER
Keep temperature between 24 to 27°C (75 to 80°F).

CHECK THE SG OF YOUR WORT
Once the SG drops to about 1.010 fermentation will be finished. Should be done fermenting in 3 or 4 days.

STRIPPING RUN
FIRST DISTILLATION

Distillation is the process of separating substances from a liquid mixture by heating, evaporating (forming a vapor), cooling and condensing vapor back into a liquid. Once the vapor is condensed back into a liquid it is referred to as the distillate. In the case of making whiskey the distillate is alcohol, primarily ethanol. The distillate produced during the whiskey making process starts off clear as water; this is true for any kind of spirit.

The stripping run has the sole purpose of getting all of the alcohol out of the wash. That includes the good stuff and the not so good stuff. Follow the steps outlined in this section and your stripping run will be a success.

STEP 1: REMOVE THE WASH FROM THE FERMENTATION BUCKET

If you fermented on the grain remove the mash bag from your fermentation bucket. This will require untying it from bucket and tying it to your 4X4 beam. Allow the wash to drain out of the mash bag. Squeezing the bag will help. If you fermented off the grain you can proceed directly to removing the wash. Next, begin ladling out the wash into a five gallon bucket with your plastic bowl. Fill the bucket about half way with wash. Pour the wash from the bucket into your still. Keep doing this until all of the wash is in the still. If you don't wish to have any lees, dead yeast, in your wash you can use a siphon to remove the wash.

STEP 2: POUR THE WASH INTO THE STILL

Each time you collect about half a bucket of wash pour it into your still. If your still is located close enough to your still you could just ladle the wash directly from the fermentation bucket. Otherwise, moving the wash to the still with a 5 gallon bucket works very well.

STEP 3: ATTACH THE HEAD ONTO THE STILL AND FASTEN THE LYNE ARM TO THE CONDENSER TUBE

Place the still head on top of the still. Fasten the lyne arm to the condenser tube. If your still has a fastening nut for connecting the head tube to the condenser tube, tighten it by hand, doesn't need to be too tight. Using the side of your hand, lightly pound the still head into place on the still. You want the still head to sit squarely onto the still with the seam even all the way around.

STEP 4: SEAL THE STILL HEAD

Mix up some flour paste and seal your still head.

STEP 5: SET UP 1 GALLON COLLECTION JAR AND ALCOHOL PARROT

For the stripping run you will use a 1 gallon jar to collect the distillate. Place the jar on a small table or small wooden box so it sits below you condenser. Place the food grade condenser collection tube into the top of your parrot. Position the parrot tube so that distillate will flow into your gallon jar from the parrot. Place your alcohol hydrometer inside the parrot as shown.

Food grade condenser tube bringing distillate from the still.

This picture shows the food grade condenser tube feeding into the top of the parrot, the correct placement of the alcohol hydrometer, and the correct positioning of the parrot so that distillate will flow into the collection jar.

Correct Still Setup

This picture shows the still placed on the burner, the lyne arm connected to the condenser tube, and the food grade tube from the condenser going into the top of the alcohol parrot. The alcohol hydrometer is correctly placed into the parrot. The parrot is positioned to allow distillate to flow into the 1 gallon collection jar.

STEP 6: TURN ON YOUR BURNER

The goal is to heat up the wash slowly. If you heat it up too fast you could burn the wash and you could vaporize the liquid too fast. This would result in too high a concentration of water coming through with your alcohol. So go slow! As the run progresses you will need to increase the temperature a little at a time. You will know it is time to increase the temperature when the distillate dripping rate slows way down. It will take about 3 hours before you see any distillate dripping from your collection tube. Then things will speed up.

STEP 7: TURN ON THE CONDENSER WATER LINE

Turn on your water line to the condenser immediately before or after turning on your burner. Just a trickle will do. The water will slowly come in through the bottom waterline and will slowly trickle out of the top outlet line. This will keep your condenser water cool enough to liquefy the vapor coming from the still. You must make sure the incoming water is cold. Also make sure your outflow line is set up to drain outside or into some kind of drain.

STEP 8: COLLECT THE DISTILLATE

You should see your first drips of distillate after about 2 to 3 hours. The vapor temperature will be around 60°C (140°F). When your parrot fills with distillate you will be able to start observing the abv. It will start at around 60%. As the temperature rises up into the 70°C (158°F) range the distillate will start to drip faster. You want fast steady dripping, not a solid stream. Once your temperature reaches around 70°C (158°F) it will quite suddenly jump up towards the 80°C (176°F) area. Try to keep the temperature around this level for as long as you can by adjusting your burner. Your beginning abv should be around 75%. The temperature will slowly increase and the abv will slowly decrease as the run continues. Monitor your abv and keep distilling until the abv has dropped to around 10%. Your vapor temperature will be around 95°C (203°F) at this point. You can distill all the way down to 0% abv, but there is not much alcohol at that point, mostly water. I recommend stopping the run at around 10% abv. The final combined abv of your distillate will be around 40%. This is called the low wines. You should get about 15 to 20% of your wash returned as low wines. Of course this will depend on when you decide to stop the run. If your final combined abv is above 40% you should add some purified water to dilute the distillate down to 30-40% abv before doing the spirit run (second distillation). You do not want to place a high abv charge into your still. 40% abv is flammable. This can be dangerous if you have a spill. The entire run for a 7 gallon wash will take about 8 hours.

Label your collection jars with the following: Stripping Run, Batch Number, Date. Keep these in a safe place until you are ready to do the spirit run.

See the data on pages 80 and 81 for an example stripping run. This data shows the vapor temperature and abv in 10 minute increments for a typical stripping run. This will give you a good example of how the temperatures and alcohol levels change as the run proceeds. There can be variations due to differences in equipment and the particular type of spirit being produced, but this data will give you some guidelines about what to expect when doing your stripping runs.

Example Stripping Run Data

Bourbon batch.
Start Time: 11:30 a.m.

Wash Volume: 6.5 Gallons

Time	ABV	Vapor Temp.	Boiler Temp.
12:00 PM	-----	-----	40°C
12:10 PM	-----	-----	50°C
12:20 PM	-----	40°C	55°C
12:25 PM	-----	43°C	60°C
12:30 PM	-----	44°C	65°C
12:40 PM	-----	48°C	70°C
12:50 PM	-----	50°C	75°C
1:05 PM	-----	55°C	80°C
1:15 PM	Slow First Drips	60°C	85°C
1:20 PM	Medium Speed Drips	65°C	87°C
1:30 PM	Medium Speed Drips	70°C	88°C
1:40 PM	Fast Drips	80°C	90°C
1:45 PM	74% abv	85°C	91°C
1:55 PM	68%	86°C	91°C
2:00 PM	64%	86°C	91°C
2:10 PM	63%	86°C	91°C
2:20 PM	62%	86°C	91°C
2:30 PM	62%	86°C	92°C
2:40 PM	61%	86°C	92°C
2:50 PM	60%	87°C	93°C
3:00 PM	59%	87°C	93°C
3:10 PM	58%	87°C	93°C
3:20 PM	57%	89°C	93°C
3:30 PM	56%	89°C	93°C

Example Stripping Run Data

Bourbon batch.
Start Time: 11:30a.m.

Wash Volume: 6.5 Gallons

Time	ABV	Vapor Temp.	Boiler Temp.
3:40 PM	53%	90°C	93°C
3:50 PM	51%	90°C	93°C
4:00 PM	51%	90°C	93°C
4:10 PM	51%	90°C	93°C
4:20 PM	50%	90°C	93°C
4:30 PM	49%	90°C	93°C
4:40 PM	48%	91°C	94°C
4:50 PM	47%	91°C	94°C
5:00 PM	46%	91°C	94°C
5:10 PM	45%	91°C	94°C
5:20 PM	43%	92°C	94°C
5:30 PM	41%	93°C	94°C
5:40 PM	40%	93°C	94°C
5:50 PM	39%	93°C	94°C
6:00 PM	39%	93°C	94°C
6:10 PM	39%	93°C	95°C
6:20 PM	37%	93°C	95°C
6:30 PM	34%	93°C	95°C
6:40 PM	32%	93°C	96°C
6:50 PM	31%	93°C	96°C
7:30 PM	25%	94°C	97°C
8:00 PM	21%	95°C	97°C
8:15 PM	17%	96°C	98°C
8:30 PM	12%	96°C	98°C

STRIPPING RUN OBSERVATIONS:

1. The vapor temperature and boiler temperature started off with a wide degree of variation.

2. As the run proceeded the vapor temperature and the boiler temperature variation narrowed.

3. It took 1.25 hours before the first slow drips of distillate were noted.

4. Fast drips, at the desired rate, began at 1:40 PM. The desired rate is about 3 drips per second. You want a steady drip, not a solid stream.

5. At 1:45 PM enough distillate was collected to be able to read the starting abv on the alcoholometer. It read 74% abv.

6. The run was stopped at 8:30 PM. The ending abv was 12% and the vapor temperature was 96°C. You could distill longer, but the distillate doesn't have much worthwhile alcohol in it at this point.

7. The combined abv of all of the distillate mixed together was 42%. About average for a stripping run.

8. Total quantity of distillate was 188 oz., about 23% of the wash volume. This is the low wines.

SPIRIT RUN
SECOND DISTILLATION

This is an overview of the spirit run. We will cover the specific step afterwards. First, clean out your still and place the distillate from the stripping run into your still. If your low wines are 40% abv or above, add a half gallon of water or so to your still. This will drop the low wines abv down into the thirties and make your distillation safer. The purpose of this run is to separate the different alcohols out and to isolate the ethanol, the good stuff, as much as possible. It is best to collect 4 ounces of distillate at a time in 8 ounce mason jars. You will need about 24 eight ounce jars and maybe more depending on the size of your batch. When the run is finished you will be able to make your cuts and separate the heads, hearts, and tails by analyzing each jar. This will be explained step-by-step on page 92. You want to heat your still slowly. You should control your burner temperature to ensure a steady drip of distillate, not a stream. If you start getting a stream, back off the heat a little bit. Three drips per second is good. Distilling too fast will make it harder to separate the different alcohols from the run.

You should see your first slow drips of distillate after about 30 minutes. The vapor temperature will be around 60°C (140°F). The first few ounces of distillate are called the foreshots. These contain methanol, which is poisonous, and other undesirable alcohols that must be discarded. There is a lot of conflicting information about the quantity of foreshots to discard. Some distillers believe foreshots should be removed from both the stripping run and the spirit run. Others believe they should be removed from one or the other. I recommend discarding one ounce per gallon of wash from the spirit run. You might be discarding a little more than you really need to, but you're just removing some early heads so it doesn't really matter; you probably don't want to keep them anyway. Better to be on the safe side. So, if we had 7 gallons of wash after fermentation, we would discard the first 7 ounces of foreshots from the spirit run. Around 5% of your distillate will be foreshots. As the run continues the temperature will rise and the abv will decline, just like in the stripping run. However, the abv will be much higher to begin with, since you are now distilling a more concentrated solution.

Within another 10 minutes or so your temperature will move up to about 70°C (158°F) and you will start seeing faster drips of distillate. At this point the distillate will be the heads of your run. The heads will normally have an abv of 80% and above. Heads can be discarded or kept and added to your next batch of low wines for distillation. The heads contain compounds like acetone, acetaldehyde, acetate and some ethanol. They have a strong, almost fruity smell and taste harsh. Approximately 20-30% of the liquid collected during a spirit distillation run will be heads.

As you continue the run the temperature will suddenly rise to about 78°C (172°F) and you will have fast dripping distillate. This is where the hearts will begin. The hearts contain mainly ethanol and are the part of the spirit run we want to collect and make into whiskey. Hearts will have a light sweet smell and a light sweet, smooth taste. Be warned though, hearts still do not taste like whiskey, they are still raw distillate. The vapor temperature, where the majority of the hearts will be boiling and vaporizing, will be between 78°C (172°F) and 82°C (179.6°F). But remember that there is still a considerable amount of ethanol coming out in your distillate at temperatures above that range, even as high as 90°C (194°F). The abv of your hearts will be below 80% and down to about 55% to 60% abv. This can vary depending on your equipment, the kind of spirit you are distilling, and many other variables. Monitoring your temperature and abv is important, but they are only a guideline for making your final cuts. The skill of the distiller is in developing the ability to smell and taste the different fractions of distillate in order to separate the heads, hearts and tails effectively. The first 4 ounces collected, in one of your 8 ounce mason jars, should have a vapor temperature of about 80°C (176°F) and an abv of about 80% (160 proof). As you continue to distill, and collect distillate in 4 ounce amounts, the vapor temperature will slowly rise and the abv will slowly decline. Eventually you will have about 24 jars each filled with 4 ounces of distillate all lined up in a row on your table. Each will be labeled with their respective temperatures and abv's. Approximately 30-40% of the run will be hearts. The temperature will continue to rise and the abv will decline. As your temperature moves past 82°C (179.6°F) the quantity of ethanol in the distillate with begin to decline.

As the temperature approaches 90°C (194°F) tails of the run will start to show up. The tails occur toward the end of the run. Tails do contain some ethanol as well as fusel oils like propanol, butanol and amyl alcohol. Tails also contain water, carbohydrates and proteins. You will know when the tails start because they smell like a wet dog and taste muddy. You may also see an oily sheen on surface of your distillate and it will start to look cloudy. Stop the run at about 96°C (205°F) or 20% abv. Tails will make up 20-30% of your run. Tails can be discarded or collected and added to the next spirit run. To make the cuts for the heads, hearts, and tails you need to consider the temperature, abv, aroma, and taste of each jar. The spirit run will take 3 to 4 hours to complete. Step 13 will explain making the cuts in more detail.

STEP 1: CLEAN YOUR STILL

After the stripping run is finished you need to clean your still. You can use alcohol or white vinegar, but don't use bleach on anything made of copper. It will corrode the copper. I recommend vinegar.

Pour about a pint of vinegar into your still, add a couple of gallons of water and scrub out your still with a dish scrubber pad. Rinse out your still 3 times with a hose. Do the same for your still head. You should also pour some vinegar through you alcohol parrot and rinse it out good.

The main thing you are getting rid of when cleaning your still is copper sulfate ($CuSO_4$). When you are distilling the vapors in the still contain sulfur. The sulfur binds with the copper your still is made of and creates copper sulfate. The copper sulfate binds to the interior of your still. This is a very beneficial reaction because it removes the sulfur from your distillate. This greatly improves the taste of your product. The only negative thing is you need to clean the copper sulfate out of your still after each use. Some vinegar, water and moderate scrubbing will do the job.

STEP 2: PUT A LINE OF DUCT TAPE ON YOUR TABLE

This will be for recording the temperature and abv for each of your small collection jars as the run progresses. It is important to collect the distillate in 4 ounce increments and record the temperature and abv. This will help you make the heads, hearts and tails cuts when the run is finished.

STEP 3: GET YOUR 8 OUNCE MASON JARS READY

Rinse out your jars and have them ready to go. Once the distillation gets going you will be filling jars and setting up new ones about every 10 minutes.

STEP 4: POUR THE LOW WINES INTO THE STILL

Take your low wines jars and pour them into your still. Your low wines should have an abv that is lower than 40%. If you have a batch of low wines that are higher than 40% abv you should add some purified water and dilute it down. Check the abv again with your alcohol hydrometer.

STEP 5: PUT YOUR STILL BACK TOGETHER

Put the still head back on. Connect the lyne arm to the condenser. Reseal the head with flour paste.

STEP 6: TURN ON THE CONDENSER WATER LINE

You want just a trickle of water coming in through your water line. The amount coming in must equal the amount going out through the outflow line on top of the condenser. The goal is to keep the water in the condenser cool.

STEP 7: SET UP FORESHOTS COLLECTION JAR

This jar will be used to collect the first 7 ounces of your spirit run (for our 7 gallon wash example). *This will include the foreshots and should be dumped.* It will contain methanol and other undesirable alcohols. *Do not use your parrot to collect this first jar.* You don't want methanol in your parrot.

STEP 8: TURN ON YOUR BURNER

For the spirit run you can start off with medium high heat and turn it down when the temperature begins to rise to about 70°C (158°F). Let the temperature rise slowly by adjusting your burner. You want each of the kinds of alcohol to boil out slowly.

STEP 9: COLLECT FORESHOTS

Remember, you are not using the alcohol parrot at this step. Collect the foreshots directly into your foreshots jar, the one you are going to dump. At about 60°C (140°F) you will start to see slow drips of distillate. It will take about half an hour for this to start. The temperature will slowly rise. Then the temperature will spike to around 78°C (172°F) and the speed of the drips of distillate will increase. You want fast dripping distillate, but not a steady stream. If you get a stream you will not be separating the different fractions of alcohol correctly. Turn the temperature down a little if this happens. When the first jar has close to 7 ounces of distillate in it get ready to pull it. I like to be on the safe side and recommend dumping 1 full ounce per gallon of wash which would be 7 ounces for our example batch. Dump this first jar and check it off on your product record sheet so you know you have completed this important step.

STEP 10: PUT THE ALCOHOL PARROT AND FIRST JAR IN PLACE AND COLLECT DISTILLATE

After discarding the foreshots put your parrot under the distillate tube from your condenser. Put your first jar under the parrot tube to collect the distillate. It will take a few minutes for the parrot to fill with distillate and start dripping. This is helpful because it gives you some time to get your next jar in place. Put your alcohol hydrometer into the parrot. As the first jar fills your still vapor temperature will be around 80°C (176°F) and your abv will be around 80%. Monitor your burner and try to keep it around 80°C (176°F). As the run continues the temperature will slowly rise and the abv will slowly drop. Monitor your burner and adjust as necessary to keep a steady drip of distillate.

STEP 11: COLLECT DISTILLATE IN 4 OUNCE QUANTITIES AND RECORD DATA

As each jar fills to about half full, 4 ounces, replace the jar with an empty one and place the full one on your table by the duct tape. Check the temperature and abv for each jar and write them on the duct tape as shown below.

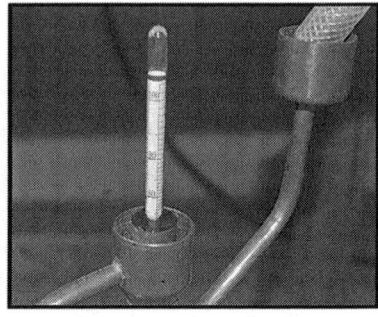

Vapor Thermometer   Alcoholometer

The picture shows a jar half full of distillate with the correct data recorded on the duct tape. This one had a vapor temperature of 81°C (177.8°F) and an abv of 80%. We are dividing the run into 4 ounce increments so it will be easier the make the heads, hearts and tails cuts when the run is finished. Keep filling your jars and recording the data until the run is finished. The picture on page 91 shows you what the run will look like as it progresses.

As the run progresses your table will look like the one in the picture. Each jar in a line with the temperature and abv recorded on the duct tape. You could end up with as many as 24 jars depending on when you decide to stop the run.

STEP 12: STOPPING THE SPIRIT RUN

There are several options for when to stop your spirit distillation run. You could continue to distill until there is zero alcohol coming out of your still, in other words, 0% abv. However, this is really not worth the effort. If you decide to distill out most of the tails in the batch and put them into your next spirit run, you could distill down to 10% abv. If you don't want to keep the tails for the next distillation, you could stop the run at the point where you think the tails have started in the run, possibly as early 65% abv if you use the 75/65 cuts. I recommend distilling until 10% abv and keeping the tails to put into the next spirit run. The reason for doing this is that there is still some ethanol in the tails that could be recovered in a subsequent run and the tails also contain esters which add unique flavors to your whiskey.

We will discuss making the cuts between heads, hearts and tails in step 13.

STEP 13: MAKING THE CUTS

Making the cuts refers to where in the spirit run you are going to make the divisions between heads, hearts and tails. There are some standard cuts that are used by commercial distillers that can be helpful in deciding where to make your cuts. The guideline I recommend is called the middle fifth cut used by the Glenmorangie Distillery in Scotland. They use a 75/65 cut. This means everything in a run that is above 75% abv is designated as heads. Everything that is below 65% abv is designated as tails. So everything from 75% to 65% abv is designated as hearts. This is considered to be a very tight cut, thereby producing a very high quality ethanol containing very little heads and very little tails. Of course, if you want a little more volume, you could use the general commercial distillery cuts of 75/55. If you do, you will need to be careful not to get too much tails in your final product or it will ruin the run.

In addition to using the abv percentage there are two even more important considerations when making your cuts, aroma and taste of the distillate. You need to smell the distillate in the jars and dip your finger in and taste them. The following information will help you make your cuts using the aroma and taste of your distillate.

Heads
Will have a strong, fruity odor and will have a strong taste with a bite. Contain acetone, acetaldehyde, acetate and some ethanol.

Hearts
Will smell light and sweet. They will have a smooth sweet taste. Contain primarily ethanol - the good stuff.

Tails
Will smell light a wet dog. They will taste muddy and awful. As soon as the tails start you will be able to smell them in your distillate. Contain fusel oils including propanol, butanol and amyl alcohol. Also contain proteins, carbohydrates, fatty acids, esters and some ethanol.

After you have made your cuts and separated out your hearts you can blend in some heads and tails to adjust the flavor of your final product to your liking. It takes time to learn how to blend distillate correctly. When first learning to distill I suggest you stick with aging your hearts without any blending. After you get some experience under your belt you could start experimenting with blending.

The skill is being able to sniff out and taste where the heads end and where the tails begin. Use the 75/65 cuts as a guide. Your actual runs may come out a little different than that, but it will give you a starting point. Some of your runs may end up with the heads cut closer to 80% abv and the tails cut closer to 50% abv. They will vary depending on the particular spirit you are making. Making cuts is a skill that takes time to learn.

This picture shows the heads cut marked on the duct tape. All of the jars with an abv more than 75% will be poured into a separate container and labeled "heads." On the other end, all jars with an abv less than 65% will be poured into a separate container and labeled "tails." The heads and tails will be added to the next spirit run of the same grain bill. That way you can distill out some more of the ethanol that remains.

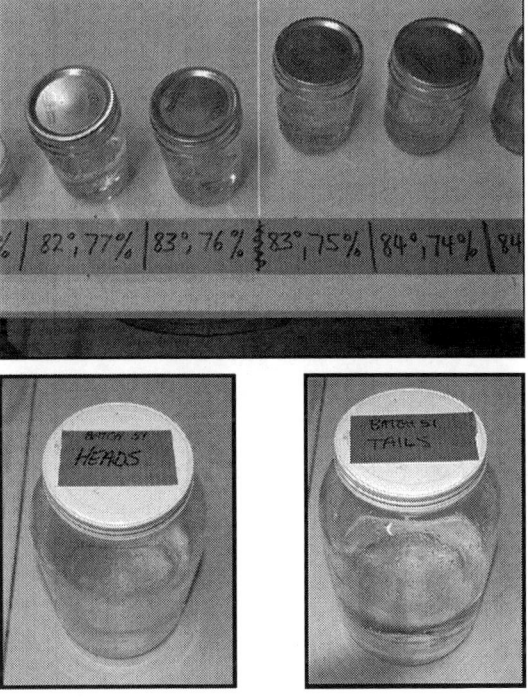

STEP 14: SEPARATE OUT THE HEARTS

Mix all of your small jars of hearts in a one gallon jar. Using a funnel, pour some hearts distillate into your graduated cylinder and measure the abv with your alcohol hydrometer. Next, measure the total volume in ounces using your measuring cup Lastly, pour all of the hearts into an aging jar. Be sure to record this information in your product record. You will need this data later on when you proof down (dilute) your final product.

A funnel was used to fill the graduated cylinder with blended hearts.

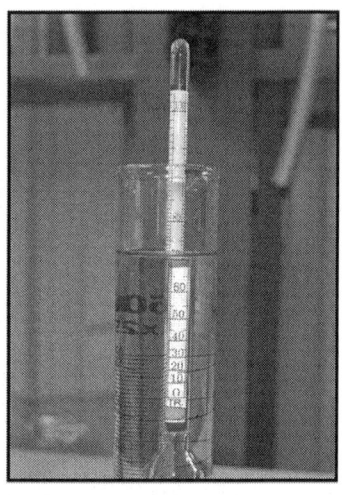

Checking the hearts abv with an alcohol hydrometer.

Measuring the quantity of hearts with a measuring cup.

Pouring hearts into a one gallon aging jar.

On pages 96 and 97 there is a complete set of data for an example spirit run. This was an actual distillation and the data is real. Study this information to get a solid understanding of the temperatures and abv percentages as the run progresses.

Example Spirit Run Data

Bourbon batch.
Start Time: 12:30 PM.   Collected in 4 ounce quantities.
7 ounces of foreshots were discarded prior to jar number 1.

Jar No.	Time	ABV	Vapor Temp.	Boiler Temp.
----	12:35 PM	----	----	50°C
----	12:37 PM	----	40°C	55°C
----	12:40 PM	----	46°C	65°C
----	12:43 PM	----	52°C	70°C
----	12:49 PM	Slow Drips	60°C	75°C
----	12:53 PM	Med. Drips	67°C	78°C
----	12:59 PM	Fast Drips	79°C	85°C
----	12:59 PM	81% abv	79°C	85°C
1	1:05 PM	81%	80°C	85°C
2	1:15 PM	80%	80°C	85°C
3	1:24 PM	80%	80°C	85°C
4	1:31 PM	77%	80°C	85°C
5	1:40 PM	77%	80°C	85°C
6	1:48 PM	77%	80°C	85°C
7	1:56 PM	77%	80°C	85°C
8	2:03 PM	77%	81°C	86°C
9	2:13 PM	77%	81°C	86°C
10	2:23 PM	76%	82°C	87°C
11	2:33 PM	74%	83°C	87°C
12	2:40 PM	73%	83°C	87°C
13	2:50 PM	71%	84°C	89°C
14	3:10 PM	69%	85°C	90°C
15	3:21 PM	68%	85°C	90°C
16	3:30 PM	66%	86°C	91°C

Example Spirit Run Data

Bourbon batch.
Start Time: 12:30 PM.   Collected in 4 ounce quantities.
7 ounces of foreshots were discarded prior to jar number 1.

Jar No.	Time	ABV	Vapor Temp.	Boiler Temp.
17	3:38 PM	63%	87°C	92°C
18	3:37 PM	57%	90°C	93°C
19	4:00 PM	51%	90°C	95°C
20	4:09 PM	46%	92°C	95°C
21	4:18 PM	40%	93°C	96°C
22	4:28 PM	37%	94°C	96°C
23	4:40 PM	20%	96°C	97°C

SPIRIT RUN OBSERVATIONS:

1. The vapor temperature and boiler temperature started off with a wide degree of variation.

2. As the run proceeded the vapor temperature and the boiler temperature variation narrowed.

3. It took 14 minutes before the first slow drips of distillate were noted.

4. Fast drips, at the desired rate, began at 12:59 PM. The desired rate is about 3 drips per second. You want a steady drip, not a solid stream.

5. At 12:59 PM enough distillate was collected to be able to read the starting abv on the alcoholometer. It read 81% abv.

6. The run was stopped at 4:40 PM. The ending abv was 20% and the vapor temperature was 96°C. You could distill longer, but the distillate doesn't have much worthwhile alcohol in it at this point.

7. The heads cut was made at jar 4, 77% abv. The cut was based on aroma and taste of the distillate.

8. The tails cut was made at jar 18, 57% abv. The cut was based on aroma and taste of the distillate.

9. Jars 4 through 18 were kept for aging.

10. Total quantity of distillate kept was 80 oz., about 43% of the low wines volume. This can vary depending on where you make your heads and tails cuts.

11. The combined abv of all of the kept distillate mixed together was 73% or 146 proof.

AGING YOUR WHISKEY

Aging your distillate is the step that actually creates whiskey. Commercial distilleries use charred oak barrels to age their product. Barrels or casks made of American White Oak wood are the most commonly used structures for aging whiskey, although there are some variations to that. Oak barrels are expensive, large (53 gallon), and take years to properly age the whiskey. An alternative to barrel aging is jar aging. This requires one gallon glass jars with lids and either charred or toasted American White Oak cubes. The process is quite simple and will create excellent product in six months or less.

First off buy some one gallon glass jars with lids. You can purchase oak cubes, but they are expensive. It is easy to get some white oak wood, cut it into small pieces and either toast it in an oven or char it with a propane torch. You can char larger amounts buy burning it on a camping stove. Put your newly distilled spirits into the jar, place a few oak chucks in, and label your jar. Your oak chucks should be about one inch square. Jar aged whiskey starts to get good after a couple of months, but I recommend letting it age for at least 6 months.

STEP 1: PROOF DOWN (DILUTE) YOUR WHISKEY TO 125 PROOF (62.5% abv)

The best proof for aging is supposed to be 125 or 62.5% abv. Although you will find some variations to that in the literature. You will need to add purified water to your whiskey in order to do this. Do not use regular tap water, it could taint the flavor of your whiskey. Use either bottled water or filtered tap water. Go to the following website for a good dilution calculator. *homedistiller.org/calcs/rad14701* Just plug in the numbers and it will show you how much water to add to your whiskey to proof it down to the desired abv.

STEP 2: POUR THE PROOFED DOWN WHISKEY INTO AN AGING JAR

STEP 3: ADD YOUR WHITE OAK CUBES TO THE JAR

Three or four one inch cubes will do the job. You can experiment with this and see what works best for you.

STEP 4: LABEL THE JAR

Photocopy and use the labels on page 26 to label your jar. Store in a safe place. Open the lid once a week to release volatile vapors.

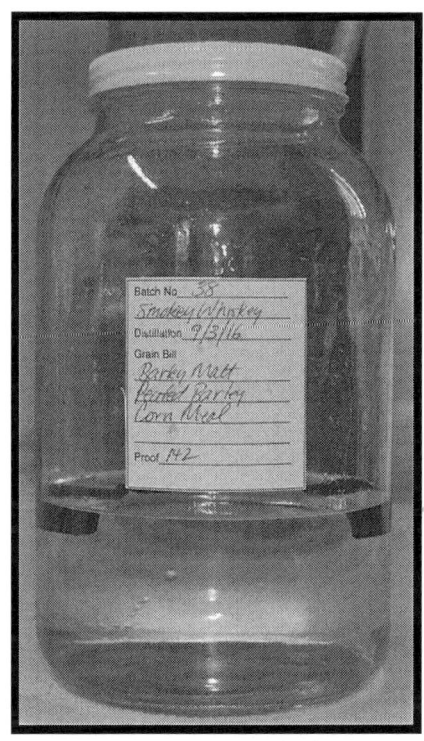

BOTTLING YOUR WHISKEY

Your whiskey will be ready to bottle when the color and taste are to your liking. It will normally take a minimum of two months. Of course, the longer you let it age the better it will be. I recommend six months for the best product. When the time arrives, get out your bottles, your funnel and some coffee filters. It is best not to filter whiskey through activated carbon of charcoal filters, they will strip out too many congeners and dilute the flavor of your whiskey.

STEP 1: PROOF YOUR WHISKEY DOWN TO YOUR DESIRED DRINKING PROOF

Decide what proof you want for your whiskey, 80, 90, etc. Measure the volume of whiskey in your jar. Some is always lost due to evaporation during the aging process. Use the dilution calculator at **http://homedistiller.org/calcs/rad14701**. Plug in the numbers and it will tell you how much water to add to your whiskey for the proof your want. Use purified water for proofing down.

STEP 2: RINSE OUT YOUR BOTTLES

STEP 3: FILTER YOUR WHISKEY INTO THE BOTTLE
   Coffee filter for whiskies, carbon filter for vodka.

STEP 4: PUT THE CORK IN

STEP 5: ATTACH YOUR LABEL

I recommend designing a label on your computer with MS Publisher. Print the label on plain paper. Cut it out and glue it onto your bottle using a glue stick. The glue stick works well and it is easy to remove the label when you need to recycle any bottles. See the examples on page 104.

Using nice bottles makes your whiskey look even better!

Filtering whiskey into a bottle. Note: This picture is black and white. The whiskey is actually a beautiful amber color!

EXAMPLE LABELS

CHAPTER 4

Recipes

Follow the instructions in chapter 3 for any of these recipes. For any recipes use the same procedures we used for our example batch.

WHISKEY

STRAIGHT BOURBON - WOODFORD RESERVE STYLE

Corn Meal 72%
Rye 18%
Barley Malt 10%
Amylase Enzyme - 1/2 teaspoon per 5 gallons mash
Yeast Nutrient - 1/2 teaspoon per gallon mash
DADY - 1/2 teaspoon per gallon mash
Yogurt (optional) - 1 teaspoon per gallon mash

SMOKEY BOURBON

Corn Meal 60%
Rye 20%
Barley Malt 15%
Peated Barley 5%
Amylase Enzyme - 1/2 teaspoon per 5 gallons mash
Yeast Nutrient - 1/2 teaspoon per gallon mash
DADY - 1/2 teaspoon per gallon mash
Yogurt (optional) - 1 teaspoon per gallon mash

WHEATED BOURBON

Corn Meal 60%
Barley Malt 20%
Rye 10%
Wheat 10%
Amylase Enzyme - 1/2 teaspoon per 5 gallons mash
Yeast Nutrient - 1/2 teaspoon per gallon mash
DADY - 1/2 teaspoon per gallon mash
Yogurt (optional) - 1 teaspoon per gallon mash
Lighter, sweeter taste than straight bourbon. (The ladies like it!)

SINGLE MALT WHISKEY
(SCOTCH WHISKY IN SCOTLAND)

Barley Malt 90%
Peated Barley 10%
Amylase Enzyme - 1/2 teaspoon per 5 gallons mash
Yeast Nutrient - 1/2 teaspoon per gallon mash
DADY - 1/2 teaspoon per gallon mash
Yogurt (optional) - 1 teaspoon per gallon mash
Typically fermented off the grain.- see chapter 3, page 69.

IRISH WHISKEY

Barley Malt 50%
Ground Barley 50%
Amylase Enzyme - 1/2 teaspoon per 5 gallons mash
Yeast Nutrient - 1/2 teaspoon per gallon mash
DADY - 1/2 teaspoon per gallon mash
Yogurt (optional) - 1 teaspoon per gallon mash
Typically fermented off the grain.- see chapter 3, page 69.

Distill 3 times - one stripping run, two spirit runs

OAT WHISKEY

Oats (quick rolled) 80%
Barley Malt 20%
Amylase Enzyme - 1/2 teaspoon per 5 gallons mash
Yeast Nutrient - 1/2 teaspoon per gallon mash
DADY - 1/2 teaspoon per gallon mash
Yogurt (optional) - 1 teaspoon per gallon mash

RYE WHISKEY (Dad's Hat Style)
Rye 80%
Barley Malt 15%
Rye malt 5%
Amylase Enzyme - 1/2 teaspoon per 5 gallons mash
Yeast Nutrient - 1/2 teaspoon per gallon mash
DADY - 1/2 teaspoon per gallon mash
Yogurt (optional) - 1 teaspoon per gallon mash

CORN WHISKEY

Corn Meal 80%
Barley Malt 20%
Amylase Enzyme - 1/2 teaspoon per 5 gallons mash
Yeast Nutrient - 1/2 teaspoon per gallon mash
DADY - 1/2 teaspoon per gallon mash
Yogurt (optional) - 1 teaspoon per gallon mash

CHOCOLATE MALT WHISKEY

Barley Malt 75%
Chocolate Barley Malt 25%
Amylase Enzyme - 1/2 teaspoon per 5 gallons mash
Yeast Nutrient - 1/2 teaspoon per gallon mash
DADY - 1/2 teaspoon per gallon mash
Yogurt (optional) - 1 teaspoon per gallon mash
The chocolate barley malt is just a darker roasted barley. There is no actual chocolate in it. The whiskey will have a subtle chocolate note.

MOONSHINE

BASIC CORN MOONSHINE

8 Gallons Water (10 gallons total mash volume)
This is for the 35 liter still. Make adjustments for the volume of your still.

Corn Meal 85%
Barley Malt 15% (needed to supply enzymes to the mash)
Amylase Enzyme - 1/2 teaspoon per 5 gallons mash
Yeast Nutrient - 1/2 teaspoon per gallons mash
DADY - 1/2 teaspoon per gallon mash

CORN AND SUGAR MOONSHINE

Corn Meal 50%
Sugar 50%
Amylase Enzyme - 1/2 teaspoon per 5 gallons mash
Yeast Nutrient - 1/2 teaspoon per gallon mash
DADY - 1/2 teaspoon per gallon mash

MALTED BARLEY MOONSHINE

Barley Malt 80%
Sugar 20%
Amylase Enzyme - 1/2 teaspoon per 5 gallons mash
Yeast Nutrient - 1/2 teaspoon per gallon mash
DADY - 1/2 teaspoon per gallon mash

SWEET FEED MOONSHINE

Sweet Feed 85%
Barley Malt 15%
Amylase Enzyme - 1/2 teaspoon per 5 gallons mash
Yeast Nutrient - 1/2 teaspoon per gallon mash
DADY - 1/2 teaspoon per gallon mash

Sweet feed is corn, oats, barley and molasses. It is sold at feed stores. Also called wet COB.

OAT MOONSHINE

Oats (quick rolled) 80%
Barley Malt 20%
Amylase Enzyme - 1/2 teaspoon per 5 gallons mash
Yeast Nutrient - 1/2 teaspoon per gallon mash
DADY - 1/2 teaspoon per gallon mash
* Similar to oat whiskey, but distilled 3 times and not aged.

INSTRUCTIONS FOR MAKING MOONSHINE

Follow the same process already covered earlier in the book for making whiskey. Just be sure to distill three times. That would be one stripping run and two spirit runs. Also, do not age the moonshine with any kind of wood and do not proof it down.

VODKA

WINTER WHEAT VODKA

Considered to be the finest vodka.
Wheat Malt 20%
Ground Red Winter Wheat 80% (Do not use white wheat)
Amylase Enzyme - 1/2 teaspoon per 5 gallons mash
Yeast Nutrient - 1/2 teaspoon per gallon mash
DADY - 1/2 teaspoon per gallon mash

INSTRUCTIONS FOR MAKING VODKA

Follow the same process already covered earlier in the book for making whiskey. Just be sure to distill three or more times if using a pot still. That would be one stripping run and two spirit runs. Do not age the vodka with any kind of wood. Polish the vodka by filtering it through an activated carbon filter and proof it down to the drinking proof, normally 80, 90, or 100 proof.

RUM

Rum is made from sugar and/or molasses. There are three main types of rum: white, gold and dark.

WHITE RUM

White rum is not aged and it is filtered which removes much of the color and flavor.

GOLD RUM

Gold rum is also known as amber rum. It is aged in charred white oak barrels.

DARK RUM

Dark rum is aged in charred white oak barrels for a longer period of time. Caramelized sugar is often added to add color and flavor.

RUM RECIPE

2 Gallons molasses
4 Lbs. Raw sugar or brown sugar
8 Gallons water
DADY - 1/2 teaspoon per gallon mash
Add caramelized sugar to aged rum. 5 to 10 tsp./quart of rum.

INSTRUCTIONS FOR MAKING RUM

1. Heat your water to 50°C (122°F).
2. Add the sugar and mix until completely dissolved.
3. Add molasses and mix well.
4. Allow the mixture to cool to 21-24°C (70-75°F).
5. Add yeast.
6. Mix and aerate.
7. Pour into fermentation bucket, put lid on.
8. Ferment at 21-24°C (70-75°F).
9. Check specific gravity every few days.
10. Fermentation may take up to two weeks to complete.
11. Distill as normal - stripping run and spirit run.
12. Age with charred white oak cubes.

SOUR MASH WHISKEY

Sour mash does not mean the whiskey tastes sour. Some of the backset from a previous distillation is used in order to help control undesirable bacteria and helps create a fuller flavored whiskey. To make a sour mash whiskey replace 1/4 to 1/3 of the required water for a new batch of mash with backset from a previous batch of the same grain bill. All of the other steps are the same.

CHAPTER 4

Cleaning and Sanitizing Your Equipment

BLEACH

Use about 1 tablespoon of bleach per gallon of water for cleaning/sanitizing your non-copper equipment. Do not use bleach on cooper items, it will corrode the metal. Use a bleach solution for your mash cooking pot, five gallon buckets, fermentation bucket and lid, mixing paddle, jars and plastic bowl. Just wipe down the items with the bleach solution and triple rinse. Rinsing three times is a good practice to make sure all of the bleach solution is removed from the item being cleaned.

WHITE VINEGAR

Use white vinegar and water to clean your still, condenser and alcohol parrot.

Outside of Still
Mix 1 tablespoon of salt, 1 cup white vinegar and enough flour to make a paste.
Apply to the outside of your still.
Let it sit for 30 minutes.
Wash off with cloth and water.

Inside of Still
Light Cleaning
A light cleaning is all that is necessary most of the time.
Put about 1 gallon of water and 2 cups of vinegar into your still.
Scrub out the still with a scrubber pad or brush.
Triple rinse.

Inside of Still
Thorough Cleaning
After every 10 distillation runs I recommend a thorough cleaning.
Put 2 gallons of water and 1/2 gallon of vinegar into your still.
Put the still head on, connect your condenser and run the still.
Heat the solution up to boiling and let it run through your system for 10 minutes.
Don't forget to set up a collection jar or you'll have hot vinegar water all over the floor.
Triple rinse.

CHAPTER 5

Safety Guidelines

Distilling spirits is actually very safe if common sense is applied. Here are some of the critical items to keep in mind when distilling.

1. DO NOT LEAVE YOUR STILL UNATTENDED.

2. USE AN ELECTRIC HOT PLATE TO HEAT YOUR STILL.
   A propane burner can be used with proper precautions.

3. KEEP YOUR CONDENSER WATER COOL.

4. HIGH PROOF ALCOHOL AND VAPOR ARE VERY FLAMMABLE.

5. DO NOT FILL YOUR STILL MORE THAN 3/4 FULL.

6. DISCARD THE FORESHOTS - THEY CONTAIN METHANOL.

7. KEEP A FIRE EXTINGUISHER NEARBY.

8. SEAL ALL LEAKS IN YOUR SYSTEM WITH FLOUR PASTE.

9. MAKE SURE TO HAVE GOOD VENTILATION.

10. USE GLASS DISTILLATE COLLECTION JARS - NEVER PLASTIC.

11. DIRECT THE DISTILLATE AWAY FROM YOUR STILL.

Expanded Glossary

Alcohols in the Distillate

There are a number of different types of alcohol produced by the yeast during fermentation. When we distill the wash the different kinds of alcohol will boil and vaporize at different temperatures. The table below shows the different alcohols that may be distilled out of a typical wash and the temperature at which each will boil. These are the temperatures at which each type of alcohol will boil if the solution is 100% pure alcohol. For example, if we had a container with 100% pure ethanol in it, it would boil and 78.4°C. When we have a typical wash containing different fractions of each kind of alcohol, the actual boiling points will be higher due to the fact that they are not in a 100% pure state. They are diluted in water. The boiling points are used as a guide to help determine when each type of alcohol is vaporized during distillation.

Product	Formula	Temp.
Acetaldehyde	C_2H_4O	20.2°C (68.4°F)
Ethyl Formate	$C_3H_6O_2$	54.3°C (129.7°F)
Acetone	C_3H_6O	56.0°C (132.8°F)
Methanol - Wood Alcohol	CH_3OH	64.7°C (1148.5°F)
Ethyl Acetate	$C_4H_8O_2$	77.1°C (170.8°F)
Ethanol	C_2H_6O	78.4°C (173.1°F)
2-Propanol	C_3H_8O	82.6°C (180.7°F)
1-Propanol - Rubbing alcohol	C_3H_8O	97.0°C (206.6°F)
Water	H_2O	100.0°C (212°F)
Butanol	$C_4H_{10}O$	117.7°C (243.9°F)
Acetic Acid	CH_3COOH	118.1°C (244.6°F)
Amyl Alcohol	$C_5H_{12}O$	131.6°C (268.9°F)
Furfural	$C_5H_4O_2$	161.7°C (323.1°F)

Alcohol By Volume (ABV)

Alcohol By Volume is usually abbreviated as ABV. It is the concentration of total alcohol, as a percentage, in the distillate or in a bottle of whiskey.
For example, 40% ABV.

Alpha-Amylase Enzyme

Alpha-amylase enzyme is an enzyme produced by germinating seeds or grain like barley. The enzyme helps break down long chained sugars (starch) into smaller carbohydrates containing one, two, or three glucose molecules. These can then be fermented by the yeast. The picture below illustrates the structure of a starch molecule. The enzyme breaks the bonds in between the glucose molecules.

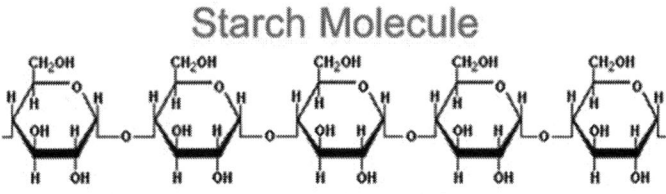

Starch Molecule
Glucose molecules bent into rings and linked together

Alcohol Hydrometer (Alcoholometer)

Hydrometer used to measure the alcohol content of a solution. The tool shows the alcohol by volume (abv), as a percentage, as well as the proof of the solution. Proof is two times the abv.

Alcohol Parrot

A copper tube that receives distillate from a still condenser and holds an alcohol hydrometer. This allows the distiller to see real-time abv readings as the distillation proceeds.

Angel's Share

The spirit lost to evaporation out of the oak barrels during aging. About 2% of the spirits are lost to evaporation each year.

Aerate

To introduce air and oxygen into something. Introducing air into the wort, for example.

Attenuation

The decline in the specific gravity of the wort as the yeast converts sugars to alcohol. Can also be expressed as the percentage of sugars the yeast consumes during fermentation.

Back Set

The wash left at the end of a stripping run that can be added into the next batch of mash. Normally used to replace 1/4 to 1/3 of the water needed in a new batch of sour mash.

Bacteria

Bacteria are microscopic single-celled organisms. There are many kinds of bacteria, some are harmful, but many are beneficial. There are several species of Lactobacillus bacteria that can enter your mash naturally or can be added intentionally. Lactobacillus will produce various acids that are used in the creation of esters in the wort. The esters will have a flavorful effect on your whiskey. You can purchase Lactobacillus bacteria to incorporate into your mash if desired.

Baking Soda

Sodium bicarbonate, $NaHCO_3$. Used to raise pH.

Beta-Amylase Enzyme

Beta-amylase is an enzyme also produced by germinating seeds or grains. The enzyme breaks chemical bonds at the end of the sugar chains (starch). This process produces two-chained sugars like maltose. It is an important process in whiskey making because is helps facilitate the saccharification process. The picture below shows a molecule of maltose which is made of two glucose molecules.

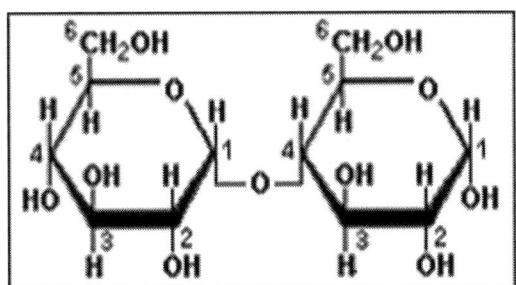

Blending

The process of carefully adding heads and or tails to a batch of hearts in order to attain a certain flavor in the final whiskey product. This takes a fair amount of skill to do correctly.

Boiling

Heating a liquid to the temperature at which it bubbles and turns to vapor. Boiling occurs below the surface of a heated liquid. Ethanol boils in relation to its concentration in water. The lower the concentration of ethanol in water, the higher the boiling temperature of the ethanol.

Cask Strength

The abv of whiskey as it is being aged in a cask. Also known as barrel proof. Aging proof is normally between 120 and 130 proof. The most popular aging proof is 125 (62.5% abv).

Charge

The charge is the amount of liquid, e.g., low wines, being placed in a still for distillation.

Congeners

Congeners are substances other than ethanol that are produced during fermentation. They can effect the flavor of the distillate positively or negatively.

Copper Sulfate ($CuSO_4$)

When distilling with a copper still, sulfur, produced by the yeast during fermentation, binds with the copper to produce copper sulfate. This is good because it removes the sulfur from your distillate. When you clean your still the copper sulfate is washed away.

Cuts

During distillation the cuts are the points at which the distiller separates the heads and the tails leaving the hearts of the run.

Cutting

Diluting whiskey by adding water. Also known as proofing down. It is customary to cut whiskey after aging is complete, since whiskey is aged at about 125 proof. This brings the proof of the whiskey down to a drinkable level.

Distillation

Distillation is the process of separating substances from a liquid mixture by heating, evaporating (forming a vapor), cooling and condensing vapor back into a liquid. Once the vapor is condensed back into a liquid it is referred to as the distillate. In the case of making whiskey the distillate is alcohol, primarily ethanol. The distillate produced during the whiskey making process starts off clear as water; this is true for any kind of spirit.

Distillate

The liquid produced from the process of distillation. In our case, ethanol plus other forms of alcohol.

Esters

Esters are compounds produced during fermentation. They result from the combination of alcohols and fatty acids or acetates. Esters add aromas and flavors to the spirit.

Important Esters in Distilling	Flavor
Butyl Acetate	Apple
Ethyl Acetate	Pear
Ethyl Butyrate	Pineapple
Ethyl Cinnamate	Cinnamon
Ethyl Hexanoate	Apple
Isoamyl Acetate	Banana
Methyl Trans-Cinnamate	Strawberry
Octyl Acetate	Orange
Propyl Acetate	Pear

Esterification

A reaction of an alcohol with an acid to produce an ester and water.

Ethanol
Ethanol, also known as ethyl alcohol, has the chemical formula C_2H_5OH and is one of the alcohols produced by yeast during sugar fermentation.

Feints
The final distillate from a spirit run. The feints are low in alcohol and can be added to the next run and redistilled.

Evaporation
Evaporation occurs at the surface of a boiling liquid as the liquid transitions into vapor.

Fermentation
Fermentation is the process of converting sugars, like glucose and maltose, into acids, carbon dioxide (CO_2), and various alcohols by yeasts. This is called glycolysis. The breakdown of glucose also releases carbon atoms which can be used by the yeast to grow and reproduce (budding). It is important to make sure the yeasts have an ample supply of oxygen and other nutrients for efficient fermentation.

Fermentation Bucket
A bucket and lid used to ferment wort.

Ferment Off The Grain
The wort is separated from the mash and fermented.

Ferment On The Grain
The entire mash, including grains and wort, is fermented.

Flocculation
Yeasts' ability to clump together at the end of a fermentation.

Foreshots
The first few ounces of distillate produced during a distillation. They contain methanol and other volatile alcohols.

Fusel Oils

Fusel oils are higher order alcohols. Fusel is a German word which means "bad liquor." They have an oily consistency, smell like a wet dog, and taste bad. Fusel oils include: propanol, butanol, amyl alcohol, and furfural.

Gelatinization

When using corn meal or polenta as your source of corn in a batch, the corn must first be gelatinized. This involves heating the corn in water which breaks the bonds between the starch molecules. This basically dissolves the starch and allows the corn to absorb more water. The mixture will become very thick. Once the corn is gelatinized you can add the remaining grains (e.g., barley malt, rye) and proceed to cook the batch.

Grain Bill

In the distilling industry the grain bill is simply a list of which grains are used to make the mash and the percentage of each. For example, the grain bill for Jack Daniels Tennessee Whiskey is 80% corn, 12% rye and 8% malted barley. Of course, trying to make Jack Daniels whiskey isn't just a matter of using their grain bill. They use various techniques in their production process that produces the unique flavors of Jack Daniels, techniques that are closely guarded secrets.

Grain Cap

The layer of grain pushed up by carbon dioxide produced by yeast during fermentation. You will see a grain cap form at the top of your fermentation bucket.

Gypsum

Calcium sulfate, $CaSO_4$. Used to lower pH.

Heads

The first major part of the distillate is called the heads. The heads contain compounds like acetone, acetaldehyde, acetate and some ethanol. They have a strong, almost fruity smell and taste harsh. Heads can be discarded or collected and added to the next spirit run. Approximately 20-30% of the liquid collected during a distillation run will be heads.

Hearts

The hearts contain mainly ethanol and are the part of the spirit run we want to collect and make into whiskey. Hearts will have a light sweet smell and a light sweet, smooth taste. The skill of the distiller is in developing the ability to smell and taste the different fractions of distillate in order to separate the heads, hearts and tails effectively. Approximately 30-40% of the run will be hearts. See Appendix A for an illustration of Heads, Hearts and Tails.

Kraeusen

Foamy head that forms on top of fermenting wort after about 4 hours of fermentation. Consists of dead yeast and proteins.

Lautering

The process of separating the wort from the mash.

Lees

The layer of dead yeast that accumulates in the bottom of the fermentation bucket or vat. Some distillers say you should distill the lees with the wash and others say the lees should be left out of the distillation. It is the distiller's choice.

Lime

Calcium carbonate, $CaCO_3$. Used to raise pH.

Low Wines

The distillate produced from the first distillation (stripping run) of a fermented wash. Usually have an abv of about 40%.

Lyne Arm

The tube going from the still head to the condenser.

Mash

Cooked mixture of grains and water.

Mash Bag

A net-like bag used to cook or ferment mash in. The bag makes it easy to remove the grain and separate out the wort from the mash.

pH

Potential hydrogen. pH measures the acidity and alkalinity of a substance. We are concerned about the pH of our mash and our wort prior to fermentation. The pH scale is a logarithmic scale that goes from 0 to 14. Seven is neutral, anything below 7 is acidic, and anything above 7 is alkaline. Acidic substances have a high concentration of hydrogen ions (H^+) and alkaline substances have a high concentration of hydroxyl ions (OH^-).

In the distilling business the optimum pH for mash is between 5.2 and 5.7, moderately acidic. This pH range improves the activity of the enzymes responsible for saccharification and gives us a better conversion of the starches in the mash to glucose. It is a good idea to check the pH of your mash with a pH test strip or a digital pH meter. The good news is that mash is naturally in the pH range of 5.2 to 5.7 because grains are acidic by nature.

The optimum pH for fermentation by the yeast is between 4.0 and 4.5. Yeast thrive in a acidic environment and are the most healthy in this pH range. This pH also helps control bacterial growth.

You should check the pH of your wort prior to fermentation. If the pH values for either your mash of your wort are high or low you can adjust them quiet easily. For a pH that is too low, too acidic, you can add calcium carbonate (lime). Mix in 1/2 teaspoon at a time. Recheck your pH. Keep adding 1/2 teaspoon at a time until you get it into the correct range. For a pH that is to high, too alkaline, add citric acid or calcium sulfate (gypsum). Mix in 1/2 teaspoon at a time. Recheck your pH. Keep adding 1/2 teaspoon at a time until you get it into the correct range.

When you check your pH levels you might find they are fine. However, there are variables that can cause your pH to be out of the correct range, one of which is your water.

Pitching Yeast

Putting yeast into the mash or the wort.

Polishing

Filtering the distillate to remove congeners. An activated carbon filter is normally used.

Potential Alcohol

This is the amount of alcohol we would expect to be produced from the fermentation of the wort. Most batches of wort will have between 8 and 10% potential alcohol.

Proof

Alcohol proof is twice the percentage of alcohol by volume. So if you have a whiskey that is 40% abv it would be 80 proof.

Rectification

The process of repeated distillation that produces a purified product. The product being ethanol in the case of spirit distillation.

Saccharification

The breaking apart of polysaccharides (complex sugars and starches) to soluble sugars like glucose is called saccharification. Malted barley containing beta-amylase enzyme, and the addition of alpha-amylase enzyme to the mash, break the starch molecules apart to produce single molecules of glucose (simple sugar). The glucose can then be consumed by the yeast during fermentation.

Single Barrel

Single barrel whiskey (or single cask whisky), is whiskey that comes from an individual aging barrel, instead of being created by blending together the contents of different barrels.

Small Batch Whiskey

Small batch whiskey is whiskey that is produced by mixing the contents of a small number of selected barrels. So, it is blended whiskey.

Single Malt Scotch

Single malt whisky made at a single distillery in Scotland.

Sour Mash
Sour mash whiskey is made by adding some backset from a previous batch to the mash of a new batch. Most bourbon made in the USA is made using sour mash, although most distilleries don't advertise the fact. Sour mash is typically made with backset contributing 1/4 to 1/3 of the total mash volume.
Sour mash helps in the following ways:
1. It reduces the pH thereby making the mash more acidic. This is known as acidification.
2. Ensuring the proper mash pH helps to control bacteria like Clostridium butyricum which can ruin the batch.
3. Increases the effectiveness of enzymes in the mash which convert starches to simpler sugars like glucose and maltose.
4. Contributes to healthier yeast since they thrive in a moderately acidic environment.
5. Can create a fuller flavor profile in the finished product.

Sparging
Sparging is a step at the end of the mashing process where hot water, 170°F (77°C), is run through the grain bed to extract more of the sugar from the grain.

Specific Gravity
In technical terms, the density of a substance divided by the density of the water. In distilling the substance would be sugar or alcohol. For example, the density of sugar divided by the density of water.

Spirit
From Aristotle, in 327 B.C., who thought drinking distilled beer or wine put spirit into the body of the drinker.

Sugar Hydrometer (Saccharometer)
Hydrometer that measures the specific gravity of a solution; the wort and/or wash in the case of whiskey production. This shows the amount of sugar in the solution which can be used to indicate the potential alcohol.

Tails

The tails occur at the end of the run. Tails do contain some ethanol as well as fusel oils like propanol, butanol and amyl alcohol. Tails also contain water, carbohydrates and proteins. You will know when the tails start because they smell like a wet dog and taste muddy. You will also see an oily sheen on top of the distillate as the tails continue to distill and the distillate will start to look cloudy. Tails can be discarded or collected and added to the next spirit run. Tails will make up approximately 20-30% of a spirit run.

Vorlauf

A German word for recirculation. The process of pouring heated wort back into the grain bed for sparging.

Wash

The wash is the liquid produced after fermentation is completed. The wash will normally contain 8 to 10% alcohol. The wash goes into the still for distillation.

White Dog

The alcohol that comes out of the still and is placed into aging barrels is called white dog. It has no color and little whiskey flavor at this point. It is the raw distillate.

Wort

The wort is the liquid produced from the mashing process. It contains glucose which will be fermented by yeast. By using a sugar hydrometer we can measure the specific gravity of the wort and determine what is known as the potential alcohol level.

Wort Chiller

A device made of copper or stainless steel tubing used to cool wort prior to fermentation. The tube is placed into a container of heated wort. A cold water source is connected to the tube. Water flows through the tube and cools the wort.

Yeast

Yeasts are microorganisms that ferment the wort and create alcohol. They are single celled microorganisms classified as members of the fungi kingdom. Saccharomyces cerevisiae is the primary species of yeast used in the distillation of spirits, however, there are many strains of yeast used within that species by the different distilleries. I recommend Distiller's Active Dry Yeast (DADY). This is a good all purpose yeast for distilling that works very well. Once you become an experienced distiller you can branch out and try different strains. Adding yeast to the mash is called "pitching" the yeast. Keep your yeast in an airtight container in the refrigerator.

Yeast Nutrients

The source of energy consumed by yeast is glucose, but yeast also requires other nutrients in order to reproduce and grow. Yeast nutrient blends contain a mix of trace elements, inorganic nitrogen, organic nitrogen, zinc and phosphates that helps yeast grow and complete fermentation. Yeast nutrients are added to the mash at the same time as the yeast is pitched.

Yogurt

Some distillers use plain yogurt or other sources of Lactobacillus bacteria in their mash recipes. It is believed that Lactobacillus will produce various acids that will be made into esters by the yeast during fermentation. These esters have a positive impact on the flavor of the spirits. Lactobacillus will also help keep bad bacteria from growing in your mash. You can experiment with this.

Yeast Energizer

Yeast energizers contain components such as diammonium phosphate, yeast hulls, magnesium sulfate, vitamin B complexes and tricalcium phosphate. Energizers are used to give a boost to a fermentation that is sluggish or stuck during the fermentation process.

APPENDIX

Appendix A

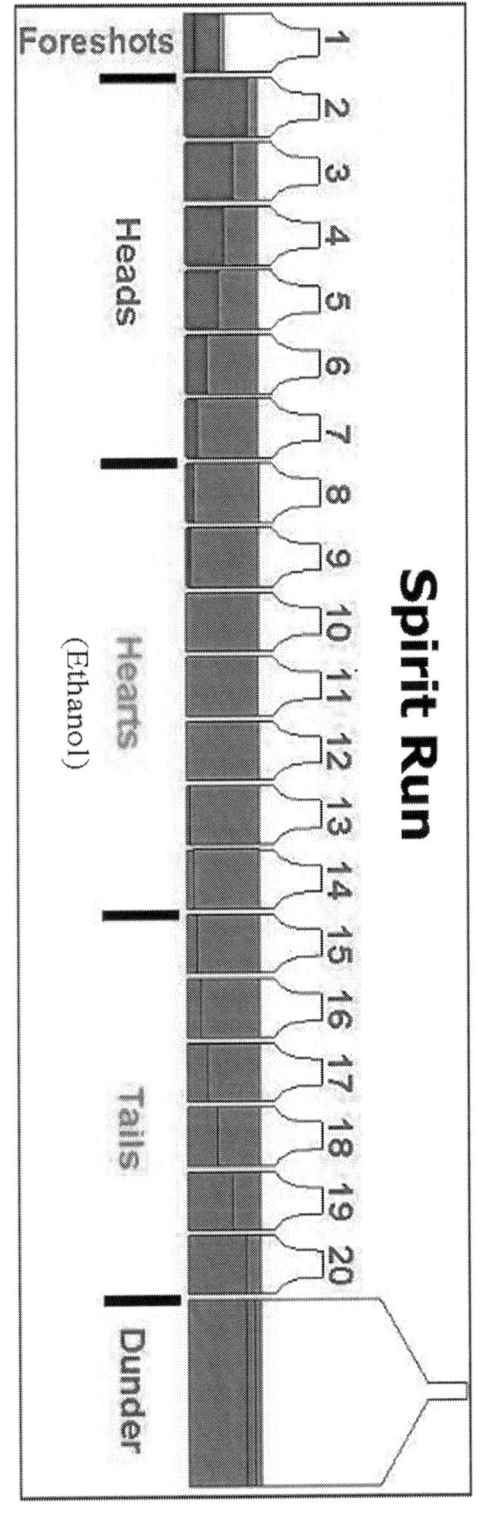

This graphic illustrates how there is ethanol in the heads and tails part of the spirit run. But, the highest concentration of ethanol is clearly in the hearts or middle part of the run.

Appendix B
Summarized Whiskey Making Instructions

1. Select your grain bill, page 47

2. Calculate mash volume, page 48

3. Calculate required grain quantities, page 50

4. Cook the mash, page 52
   - Put water into cooking pot
   - Heat water to 75°C (167°)
   - Add corn
   - Gelatinize corn 1 hour
   - Heat back to 70°C (158°F)
   - Add remaining grains
   - Add amylase enzyme
   - Mix well
   - Check mash pH
     - optimum for starch conversion, 5.2 - 5.7
   - Rest at 64.4°C (148°F) for 90 minutes
   - Cool the mash to 24° - 27°C (75° - 80°F)
   - Check and record specific gravity and potential alcohol

5. Fermentation on the Grain, page 56
   - Check the pH of your mash
     - optimum for yeast health, 4.0 - 4.5
   - Sanitize equipment
   - Place mash bag into fermentation bucket
   - Put yeast nutrients into mash pot, mix
   - Pitch yeast, mix

- Aerate mash with 5 gallon buckets three times
- Pour mash into fermentation bucket
- Put lid on fermentation bucket and label
- Put fermentation bucket in fermentation chamber
- Turn on space heater
- Procedures During Fermentation
    - Check batch for grain cap and crackling sound after about 3 hours
    - Check fermentation chamber temperature each day
    - Check SG after 3 days
- Recovering the Wash
    - Open fermentation bucket
    - Tie rope around top of mash bag
    - Pull fermentation bucket underneath your 4X4 beam
    - Tie the mash bag to the 4X4 beam
    - Let the mash bag drain and squeeze/press out the wash

6. Fermentation Off the Grain, page 69
    - Cool the mash
    - Sanitize all of your equipment
    - Separate the wort from the mash
    - Tie up the mash bag to your 4X4 beam and allow to drain
    - Squeeze/press out remaining wort
    - Sparge the mash (optional)
    - Pour all of the wort into a fermentation bucket
    - Check and record specific gravity and potential alcohol
    - Check pH
        - optimum for yeast health, 4.0 - 4.5
    - Add yeast nutrients
    - Pitch yeast - mix
    - Aerate
    - Place in fermentation chamber
    - Turn on heater
    - Procedures During Fermentation
        - Check for the fizzing sound
        - Check fermentation chamber temperature each day
        - Check SG after 3 days

7. Stripping Run - 1st Distillation, page 74
   - Remove the wash from the fermentation bucket
   - Pour the wash into your still
   - Attach head onto still
   - Connect lyne arm to condenser
   - Seal the still head with flour paste
   - Set up 1 gallon collection jar and a alcohol parrot
   - Turn on burner
   - Turn on water line to condenser
   - Collect distillate until 10% abv

8. Spirit Run - 2nd Distillation, page 83
   - Clean your still
   - Put a line of duct tape on your table
   - Get 8 ounce jars ready
   - Pour low wines into your clean still
   - Attach head onto still
   - Connect lyne arm to condenser
   - Seal still head with flour paste
   - Turn on water condenser line
   - Set up foreshots collection jar - no parrot
   - Turn on burner
   - Collect foreshots - discard
   - Put parrot in place
   - Place alcohol hydrometer into parrot
   - Put first 8 ounce collection jar in place
   - Continue colleting distillate in 4 ounce quantities
   - Record temperature and abv on duct tape for each 4 ounce jar
   - Stop the run when tails begin
   - Make your cuts - heads, hearts, tails
   - Measure the abv of the collected hearts
   - Measure the quantity of hearts
   - Pour all of the hearts into a one gallon aging jar

9. Aging Your Whiskey, page 99
   - Proof your whiskey down to 125 proof (62.5% abv)
   - Pour whiskey into aging jar
   - Add toasted or charred American White Oak cubes
   - Label jar

10. Bottling Your Whiskey, page 102
    - Proof your whiskey down
    - Rinse out your bottles
    - Filter whiskey into bottles using coffee filter (carbon filter for vodka)
    - Put cork in bottle
    - Attach label to bottle

Appendix C
Equipment and Supply List

Alembic Pot Still and Parts (35 liter/9 gallon recommended)
1/2" Black Irrigation Tubing
1/2" Hose Clamps (3)
1/2" Food Grade Tubing
Alcohol Parrot
1 Gallon Distillate Collection Jar s (2)
Alcohol Hydrometer
Sugar Hydrometer
Graduated Cylinder
15 Gallon Cooking Pot with Lid
Large Wooden Stirring Paddle
Food Grade Long Stem Thermometer
Large Propane Burner - for cooking mash
5 Gallon Propane Tank
Electric Hotplate Burner - for distilling
8 Ounce Canning Jars (24)
1 Gallon Aging Jars (several)
Aging Jar Labels
Distiller's Active Dry Yeast (DADY)
Yeast Nutrients
Amylase Enzyme
Gypsum
Citric Acid
Calcium Carbonate (Lime)
American White Oak Cubes - Toasted or Charred, Purchased or Home Made
Propane Torch or Propane Camp Stove for Charring
12 Gallon Fermenting Bucket with Lid
Mash Bag
Food Scale
Large Plastic Bowl
Flour
Kitchen Strainer
Turkey Baster
Fermentation Chamber (Optional)

Space Heater with Thermostat
5 Gallon Bucket (2)
Storage Tub with Lid
Plastic Garbage Can with Lid
Plastic Funnel
pH meter or test strips
16 gallon plastic tub - for mash press
Greenhouse bench top or similar - for mash press
2X2 foot piece of plywood - for mash press
Shop Rags
Rope (10 feet)
4X4, 8 Foot
Duct Tape
Food Tongs
Sharpie
Coffee Filters
16 Ounce Measuring Cup
Cleaning Station, Hose
Bleach
White Vinegar (Gallon)
Scrubber Pads
Product Record, Notebook

INDEX

ABV temperature correction, 16-17
Aerate, 116
Aerating the mash, 59
Aerating the wort, 73
Aging jar labels, 25-26
Aging jars, 25
Aging whiskey, 99
Alcohol by volume (abv), 116
Alcohol hydrometer, 13, 116
Alcohol parrot setup, 76, 89
Alcohol parrot, 12, 116
Alcoholometer, 13
Alcohols in the distillate, 115
Alembic pot still, 10
Alpha-amylase enzyme, 53, 116
American white oak cubes, 28
Amylase enzyme, 28, 53
Angel's share, 116
Appendix, 128
Attenuation, 117

Back set, 117
Bacteria, 117
Barley malt, 6
Barley, 6
Beta-amylase enzyme, 117
Blending, 118
Boiling, 118
Bottling whiskey, 102
Bourbon, 2
Bourbon recipes, 105-106

Canning jars, 24
Cask strength, 118
Charge, 118

Charring times, 32
Chocolate male whiskey recipe, 107
Cleaning and sanitizing equipment, 112-113
Cleaning and sanitizing equipment, 57
Collecting distillate, 79, 90
Collection jar setup, 76
Condenser, 11
Congeners, 118
Cooking pot, 22
Cooling mash, 54, 69
Copper sulfate, 118
Corn whiskey recipe, 107
Corn whiskey, 2
Corn, 7
Cuts, 92, 118
Cutting, 119

Distillate collection, 79
Distillate, 119
Distillation, 119
Distiller's active dry yeast (DADY), 27, 58
Duct tape, 41

Equipment and supply list, 134-135
Esterification, 119
Esters, 119
Ethanol, 120
Evaporation, 120
Example bourbon grain bill, 48

Feints, 120
Fermentation, 56

Fermenting on the grain, 56
Fermenting off the grain, 69
Fermentation chamber, 38, 61
    temperature, 62
Flocculation, 120
Flour, 36
Food scale, 35
Food thermometer, 22
Foreshots, 120
    collecting, 89
Fusel oils, 121

Gelatinization, 121
Gelatinize corn, 52
Glucose, 5
Graduated cylinder, 21
Grain, 4
    adding to mash, 53
    anatomy, 5
    grain bill, 8, 47, 121
    grain cap, 62, 121
    grain quantities – how to calculate, 50
Gramineae, 4
Gypsum, 121

Heads, 121
Hearts – separating, 94
Hearts, 122
Homemade American white oak aging cubes, 29
Hot plate burner, 24

Irish whiskey, 2
Irish whiskey recipe, 106

Kitchen strainer, 35
Kraeusen, 122

Labels, 104

Lautering, 122
Lees, 122
Lime, 122
Low wines, 122
Lyne arm, 122

Making whiskey, 47
Maltose, 5
Maltotriose, 5
Mash, 51, 122
    aerating, 59
    cooling, 54
    mash bag, 34, 122
    mash press, 39
    mash volume – how to calculate, 48
    resting, 54
    steps for cooling, 52-55
    Meniscus, 14
Miscellaneous supplies, 45-46
Moonrakers, 3
Moonshine, 2
Moonshine recipes, 108-109

Oats, 7
Oat whiskey recipe, 107

Parrot, 12
Peat, 7
Peated barley, 7
pH, 53, 123
    of the mash, 53, 56
    of the wort, 72
    meter, 40
Plastic bowl, 35
Polishing, 123
Pot still, 10
Potential alcohol, 18, 20, 124
Pressing out wash, 68
Pressing out wort, 70

Product record, 42, 43-44
Proof, 124
Proofing down, 99
Propane burner, 23
Propane camp stove charring, 31
Propane torch charring, 30

Recipes, 105
Rectification, 124
Rum, 3
Rum recipe, 110
Rye whiskey, 3
Rye, 7
Rye whiskey recipe, 107

Saccharification, 124
Saccharometer, 18, 125
Safety guidelines, 114
Sanitizing equipment, 57, 69
Sealing still head, 76
Separating wort from mash, 69
Single barrel, 124
Single malt whiskey, 3
Single malt recipe, 106
Single malt Scotch, 124
Small batch whiskey, 124
Sour mash whiskey, 111, 125
Sparging the mash, 70, 125
Specific gravity – checking wort, 55, 71
Specific gravity, 18, 20, 55, 63, 125
Spirit run, 83
   cleaning still for, 85
   collecting foreshots, 89
   duct tape on table, 86
   eight-ounce mason jars, 86
   example spirit run data, 96
   first collection jar, 89
   foreshots collection jar, 88
   four ounce quantities, 90
   table, 96-97
   making cuts, 92
   pouring low wines into still, 87
   separating out the hearts, 94
   stopping, 91
   spirit run data table, 96-97
   spirit run graphic, 129
Spirit, 125
Still setup, 77
Stirring paddle, 23
Stripping run data table, 80-81
Stripping run, 74
Sugar hydrometer, 18, 125

Tails, 126
Tennessee whiskey, 4
Turkey baster, 37

Vodka, 4
Vodka recipe, 109
Vorlauf, 126

Wash, 126
   checking specific gravity, 63
   pressing out, 68
   recovering for distillation, 65
Wheat, 8
Whiskey, 1
Whiskey making instructions – summarized, 130
Whiskey recipes - structure of, 49
White dog, 126
Wort chiller, 40, 54, 126

Wort, 126

Yeast, 127
    pitching, 58, 72, 123
    energizer, 127
    nutrients – adding, 28, 57, 72, 127
Yogurt, 127

About the Author

Chris Yorke has a Bachelor of Science Degree in Agriculture and a Bachelor of Arts Degree in Economics from Washington State University, Pullman, WA. He also has a Masters Degree in Technical Education from City University, Seattle, WA. Chris taught High School Agriculture Science, Animal Science, Agricultural Biology and Horticulture for 32 years in SW Washington State.

Chris learned the distilling process at a licensed craft distillery in Washington State and has many years of successful distilling experience.

Made in the USA
Columbia, SC
19 January 2019